To Pres. Clark:

Political Scientists _do_
have more fun—

Best regards,
Bob Spitzr 2/2/87

D1373804

The Right to Life Movement and Third Party Politics

Recent Titles in
Contributions in Political Science
Series Editor: Bernard K. Johnpoll

The Right to Life
Movement and
Third Party Politics

ROBERT J. SPITZER

CONTRIBUTIONS IN POLITICAL SCIENCE,
NUMBER 160

GREENWOOD PRESS

NEW YORK
WESTPORT, CONNECTICUT
LONDON

Library of Congress Cataloging-in-Publication Data

Spitzer, Robert J., 1953–
  The Right to Life movement and third party
politics

  (Contributions in political science, ISSN 0147–1066 ;
no. 160)
  Bibliography: p.
  Includes index.
  1. Right to Life Party. 2. Pro-life movement—New
York (State) 3. Third parties (United States politics)
I. Title.
JK2391.R542N77 1987   324.2747'09   86–14209
ISBN 0–313–25390–0 (lib. bdg. : alk. paper)

Copyright © 1987 by Robert J. Spitzer

All rights reserved. No portion of this book may be
reproduced, by any process or technique, without the
express written consent of the publisher.

Library of Congress Catalog Card Number: 86–14209
ISBN: 0–313–25390–0
ISSN: 0147–1066

First published in 1987

Greenwood Press, Inc.
88 Post Road West, Westport, Connecticut 06881

Printed in the United States of America

The paper used in this book complies with the
Permanent Paper Standard issued by the National
Information Standards Organization (Z39.48–1984).

10 9 8 7 6 5 4 3 2 1

To
Peg Murphy
and women who have faced
similar travails

\

CONTENTS

EXHIBITS

TABLES

FIGURES

PREFACE

Abortion is, to many, a touchy subject. Therefore, unlike research on most other political subjects, the asking of questions and prodding for information often not only raised eyebrows, but prompted the suspicion-shrouded question, "How do *you* feel about abortion?" I confess here only to having opinions on the subject.

As I stated often, my concerns and motivations related to this project were and are those of a social scientist interested in learning more about an unusual and fascinating form of political expression, though it is not difficult to understand the suspicions of those on both sides of this issue. Whether one has personal opinions or not, "objectivity" is an unrealistic goal; being fair-minded is not.

I would thus like to thank those leaders and members of the Right to Life Party who responded to questionnaires or assented to interviews, and particular thanks are due those who overcame suspicions or doubts to do so. Needless to say, their input was essential.

Two research grants helped support this work. The first came from the SUNY College at Cortland Faculty Research Program, the second from a SUNY-wide University Awards Research Program Grant. Sadly, SUNY administrators have since decided to terminate this latter program. I hope that this book in some small way testifies to the folly of that decision.

Many of the findings and arguments presented in this book were developed through the preparation and delivery of conference papers at the annual meetings of the American Political Science Association and the New York State Political Science Association. I am grateful for having had these opportunities, and for the thoughtful comments and suggestions they engendered.

I wish to acknowledge the special and excellent assistance of Teri Ortolani, my then-undergraduate research assistant, for her careful work. A former colleague, Peri Schwartz-Shea, now of the University of Utah at Salt Lake City, exhibited patience and skill far above and beyond the call of duty in providing assistance related to data processing and analysis. My friend Jack Moran read an early version of the entire manuscript, offering numerous insightful comments and suggestions. I also wish to acknowledge an intellectual debt of gratitude to my former undergraduate mentor, John W. Ellwood.

In addition, my thanks to Jinny and Bill Spitzer, Ang Pedone of the Oneida County Board of Elections, all of the helpful women at the Cortland County Board of Elections, Donna Curtin for her excellent graphics work, and especially Loretta Padavona for her always first-rate secretarial work. Finally, I would like to thank Greenwood Press, and especially Mildred Vasan, for their promptness and professionalism.

INTRODUCTION

On August 13, 1982, Dr. Hector Zevallos and his wife, Rosalie Jean, were kidnapped from their home near Edwardsville, Illinois. They were held by three captors for eight days in a concrete bunker, during which time they were repeatedly interrogated and threatened with death. After the couple was released unharmed, the three abductors were arrested. The leader of the group, Don Benny Anderson, was sentenced to 30 years in prison.

The motive for the abduction was not money. Though Dr. and Mrs. Zevallos possessed some personal wealth, their home possessions were left untouched, as were their two Mercedes Benz cars. The motive for the kidnapping became clear, however, when authorities learned that the Zevalloses ran an abortion clinic in nearby Granite City. Identifying themselves as the "Army of God," the kidnappers issued a series of "epistles" which centered on their objections to abortion and, in particular, called on President Reagan to publicly denounce abortion and call for an end to the practice. At the trial of the three, the defense lawyer made opposition to abortion the keystone of his defense. Addressing the jury, he said that the three men "had a sincere, firm, honest belief that abortion is wrong and that by their acts, abortion could be brought to an end in this country. I'm not saying the Zevalloses deserved to be in that bunker . . . even though some people might believe that because of the horrible business he is in."[1]

By anyone's standards, these actions represent the most ex-

treme fringe, and were decried by abortion opponents as well
as others. Nevertheless, these actions also carry political import
that presage the political volatility of this single-issue cause.
Political violence is a relative rarity in American politics, yet it
has been a very visible, though certainly fringe, part of the movement. Other fringe activities related to the anti-abortion cause
have also grabbed headline attention, from the firebombing of
abortion clinics to the harassment of clinic employees, Planned
Parenthood officials, and prospective clients.

The point is *not* that lawless acts somehow typify the right-
to-life movement; rather, it is that few issues in American politics
have ever inspired similar extremism. The comparative infre-
quency of political violence in our history underscores the potency of the abortion issue, and directly confronts the political
system's responsiveness to new issues. If we assume that political violence—even if sporadic—represents a breakdown of
conventional means of political expression, then the larger
movement of which it is a part warrants the most careful and
methodical analysis.

This book will therefore examine a significant (and certainly
nonviolent) component of the right-to-life movement that arose
through the work of individuals who formerly had no particular
interest in politics but were moved to political action by liberalized abortion practices. This organization, the New York-based
Right to Life Party (RTLP) is in many ways symbolic of how the
abortion issue has mobilized those who, the standard wisdom
suggests, are the *least* likely to be mobilized to political action.
The ability of the abortion issue to do just this makes it both
compelling and important as a focus of study.

To gain a broader perspective on the nature of single-issue
parties, and how the political system has responded in the past,
Chapter 1 will examine other single-issue parties. As these cases
will make clear, not only is the single-issue minor party not a
recent phenomenon on the electoral scene, but the RTLP is re-
markably similar to such past parties, despite significant differences between the electoral landscape of the last century and
that of today. Though these parties were small and usually short-
lived, they played an important role in raising salient issues not

addressed by the major parties, and they also served as an important outlet for political expression.

The succeeding chapters will explore the origins, composition, and consequences of the apparently unusual and certainly controversial RTLP. But the significance of this study extends beyond the admittedly interesting details of the party. Chapter 2 examines the genesis and development of the party—but does so through the application of a dynamic model of party development that encompasses not only the social discontent giving rise to the party, but also the unique features of New York law governing political-party behavior. Chapter 3 focuses more closely on the leadership and membership of the party, relying primarily on a survey of each. Chapter 4 draws back from this particular party to make some observations and recommendations about party politics in America, drawing from the unusual New York system. This chapter argues specifically for the encouragement of a nationwide multi-party system like that of New York, as a way of promoting party renewal. If the New York system can withstand an atypical party like the RTLP (that is, a single-issue party unwilling to engage in customary partisan bargaining and compromise), so too can national parties. The advantages of such "gadfly" parties are also explored, as are some of the "myths" of two-party enthusiasts.

What follows, then, is the exploration of two political vectors—the volatile single issue of abortion, and party politics. Their point of intersection is the RTLP.

NOTES

1. "Abortion Foe Is Convicted in Couple's Abduction," *New York Times*, January 28, 1983.

1
SINGLE-ISSUE PARTIES IN AMERICAN HISTORY

Casting the light of history on contemporary occurrences does much to illuminate both past and present. In the case of political analysis, historical perspective can help rectify analytic myopia, lend continuity to apparent idiosyncrasy, and reveal intricacy in seemingly formless phenomena.

This chapter will examine four single-issue parties, all originating in the nineteenth century. In doing so, it will constitute a unique and detailed comparison of the single-issue thrust in the electoral realm. The fact that none of the cases considered here occurred in the twentieth century (although the Prohibition Party still exists today) is not a matter of mere chance. By at least one accounting, the likelihood of issue-centered minor parties, as opposed to candidate-centered parties, declined in this century because of a similar shift in emphasis from parties and party organizations to candidates as the pivot points for the major parties.[1] Clearly, the freewheeling nature of electoral politics in the nineteenth century has not continued to the present. At the same time, however, single-issue movements are no less prevalent in this century than the last. Structural and other changes have merely channeled these political energies into other outlets. The movements themselves, and their underlying bases, remain interesting and important; and the presence of a modern-day single-issue party (even one with a modest geographical base, such as the Right to Life Party) suggests the desirability, if not the intellectual necessity, of comparison with past similar parties.

Each of the four significant past single-issue parties—the Liberty Party, Free Soil Party, Greenback Party and Prohibition Party—will be examined for commonalities, which will then be summarized at the end of the chapter. The subsequent chapters on the RTLP will provide ample fodder for comparison. As mentioned in the Introduction, the analysis of the RTLP will be conducted by employing a model of party development. The model will not, however, be applied to these far briefer cases. To attempt to do so, though desirable in principle, would be undesirable for this project, given its preeminent concern with the abortion issue, and also given the added research that would otherwise be necessary to do justice to both the framework and the cases themselves. What follows is a consideration of America's most significant past single-issue parties.

THE ANTISLAVERY PARTIES

Single-issue fervor has cropped up periodically in American history; yet, no other single issue had greater impact on American politics than that of slavery, as the cataclysmic events of the Civil War starkly verify. Though only one component of the larger movement, these single-issue antislavery minor parties played a key role in bringing this issue to the attention of the major parties, and to the country as a whole.

THE LIBERTY PARTY

The first antislavery party was forged from elements of various antislavery societies in the 1830s. If it was in these groups that the movement was forged, then its master blacksmith was William Lloyd Garrison. Through his publication the *Liberator*, Garrison issued a moral call to arms against slavery that conjoined many who shared his perspective. In demanding the immediate abolition of slavery, he served both as a lightning rod for criticism on the issue, and as a force working to legitimize what was, at the time, a radical position. Garrison helped to form the New England Antislavery Society, which was followed by the American Antislavery Society in 1833.[2]

Central to the Society's actions was a petition drive aimed at

Congress to abolish slavery in the District of Columbia, as this was recognized at the time as one of the few areas where the U.S. Congress could act. (Despite Garrison's rhetoric, there was general acknowledgement at the time that the principle of federalism prevented the federal government from tampering with slavery in the slave states.[3]) Yet in 1836, the Democratic-controlled House of Representatives passed a resolution tabling this and other petitions to limit slavery. This congressional gag rule persisted until 1844 and was symptomatic of the growing sense that the major parties were utterly unwilling to deal with the slavery question.[4] As one antislavery activist ruefully observed, the Whigs and Democrats picked candidates for office "as little fit for us to support as they think we can be induced to vote for."[5] Major-party intransigence did much to prompt the Society's entrance into the partisan arena.

Grassroots sentiments coalesced around the antislavery issue early. Groups cropped up in New York, Ohio, New Hampshire, Pennsylvania, New Jersey and Michigan. In New York especially, local activism was evidenced when activists set up their own parties in many counties around the state.[6]

Finally, in November of 1839, a faction of the American Antislavery Society met in Warsaw, New York. A previous convention held in Albany in July had yielded a disappointing turnout. This time, however, the 500 attending delegates agreed on the formation of a party. Its nominees for president and vice-president, James G. Birney of New York and Francis Lemoyne of Pennsylvania, initially declined to run but assented after a follow-up party convention in 1840. Birney's nomination was met with ambivalence by some party leaders, as he was not considered to be as effective and well-known as other possible nominees. Birney was, however, a solid supporter of the cause.[7]

The party's 1840 platform called for the end of slavery in the District of Columbia and other federal territories, as well as the end of interstate slave trade. In retrospect, these objectives appear modest, especially in comparison to Garrisonian rhetoric of the time. Yet the judgment that Liberty Party goals were modest[8] underestimates the efforts of this party, their moral commitment to the antislavery movement, and the temper of the times.

As mentioned previously, agreement was nearly universal that existing states had the constitutional right to deal with slavery in their own ways, free from federal interference. Garrison challenged this view, but also challenged the very morality and legitimacy of the Constitution.[9] The very concept of abolition— abolishing slavery everywhere, forthwith—was abhorred even by most opponents of slavery. One analyst observed that calling someone an abolitionist during this time was the equivalent of being labeled a Communist in the 1950s.[10] In fact, the positions taken by the Liberty Party were very much in the forefront of the antislavery movement. For example, the party was first to oppose the annexation of Texas, viewing it as an excuse to extend slavery.[11] Also, the strong commitment to actions and proposals deemed constitutional and legal was consistent with this attempt to operate within the system. They hoped to attempt to amend the Constitution later on when broadened support would make this possible. The abolitionist antislavery societies were freer to espouse abolition sentiment on a purely moral/religious basis, unencumbered by political considerations.[12] "The Liberty Party therefore directed its efforts toward hedging in slavery, depriving it of special favors, and stimulating emancipationist sentiment within the slave states."[13] The principal purpose of the Liberty Party was succinctly stated in 1845: "to divorce the National Government from Slavery; to prohibit slaveholding in all places of exclusive national jurisdiction; to abolish the domestic slave trade, . . . and in all proper and constitutional modes to discourage and discontinue the system of work without wages."[14]

The party's concern with political considerations did not obscure its fundamentally moral motivations, and it would be a mistake to conclude that moral/religious fervor did not underlie the activities and beliefs of party adherents. As one party activist observed, "Our cause is a plain one . . . perseverance in what we believe right, wholly irrespective of results."[15] As the party's presidential nominee, James G. Birney, said, "The Liberty Party . . . was organized not for the sake of conferring office on particular men, but for the sake of freeing our country from the crime of slavery."[16]

Religious convictions and church support were instrumental not only to the antislavery movement but to the party specifically. The party's 1840 convention, for example, included a large number of ministers and clergy of various denominations.[17] Not surprisingly, biblical quotes laced party publications.[18] The appeal to churches specifically was exemplified by a pamphlet written by Birney in 1840 entitled "The American Churches, the Bulwarks of American Slavery."[19] Party stalwarts did indeed view themselves as "Stewards of the Lord."[20]

The active involvement of clergy and others sharing similar convictions and backgrounds was all the more remarkable given the prevailing low regard for politics (and especially party politics) during this time. Anti-party sentiment was pervasive in the country during this time, to such an extent that the very act of entering the partisan realm was perceived by many as the equivalent of bargaining with the devil.[21] Many in the antislavery movement feared that entrance into party politics would obfuscate the moral/religious basis of the movement. But, others argued, if slavery was indeed a sin, the primary moral obligation was to use *all* means available to defeat it.[22]

Despite the overriding concern with slavery as a sinful institution, the Liberty Party included among its number many who had experienced and knew practical politics. Indeed, many in the party were disaffected Whigs and Democrats. Thus, as the party struggled, with little success, to acquire some electoral respectability, elements within the party began to push more and more vigorously for a change in emphasis from moral/religious to economic arguments against slavery. They hoped to win adherents and broaden party support by arguing that slavery was detrimental to white workers. Though this appeal gained greater currency as the 1840s wore on, it never supplanted (nor did it take precedence over) the fundamental underlying moral appeal and motivation.[23]

The very characteristics of the Liberty Party's formation and rise described to this point occurred, as the description implies, under conditions of considerable controversy within the movement. Commenting on the key role the Liberty Party played in swinging the presidential election of 1844 to James K. Polk by depriving Henry Clay of New York's electoral support (Liberty candidate Birney drew crucial votes from Clay), journalist and abolitionist Horace Greeley wrote:

You third party wire-workers forced this man [Polk] upon us instead of the only anti-Texas candidate who could possibly be elected. On your guilty heads shall rest the curse of unborn generations! Riot in your infamy and rejoice in its triumph but never ask us to unite with you in anything.[24]

In both of his tries for the presidency, Birney faced "more opposition from antislavery friends than from rival parties."[25] Probably the party's greatest critic was abolitionist founder William Lloyd Garrison. He and most abolitionists at first were convinced that entrance into party politics would subvert the moral ascendency of their movement, as well as alienate church supporters, cultivate corruption, enrage the major parties and promote mischief.[26] Many of these suspicions dissipated as the 1840s wore on. Nevertheless, suspicions and accusations persisted. Member of the Liberty Party also harbored suspicions, and in fact were always wary of any move toward merger with other antislavery groups, even when this became inevitable in 1847 and 1848.[27]

Conflict was to be found not only between elements of the antislavery movement, but within the party itself. Throughout its 1840 and 1844 campaigns, the Liberty Party maintained its overt single-issue devotion.[28] But throughout this period, debate raged between two factions in the party. The prevailing faction espoused single-minded devotion to the slavery issue, urging neutrality towards all other issues (though the pressure to expand to other issues escalated over time).[29] Unsuccessful attempts were made to deal with such issues as the tariff, banking, and internal improvements. Even presidential candidate Birney found it "impossible to be a candidate without expressing himself on all issues of current interest."[30]

Numerous attempts were made to broaden issue concerns of the party. Both opponents (the "diehards") and proponents (the "coalitionists") of broadening the party's agenda agreed that the single-issue thrust of the party limited its growth. But the diehards argued that the party could still remain both effective and pure if it retained its narrow focus. Not surprisingly, the attempt to broaden the party at its 1846 convention was beaten back because of the influence of the party's antislavery clergy members.[31] The coalitionists did, however, succeed in promoting economic arguments against slavery, supplementing if not supplanting purely moral appeals.[32]

By 1847, various leaders and activists had become disgusted with the narrow approach of the party. They sought to unite with others who shared antislavery sentiments regardless of party.[33] This split was instrumental in the demise of the Liberty Party and the rise of Free Soil. Factionalism notwithstanding, the party might have lasted longer had its electoral fortunes not been so disappointing.

Presidential candidate Birney's vote total in 1840 was a paltry 7,000 votes. The party's vote total was depressed due to lack of organization (printed ballots were not available in many locations, for example) and also to the fact that Birney spent the entire campaign season in England. In addition, most antislavery voters were persuaded to support Whig William Henry Harrison, as the "lesser-of-two-evils" candidate. Unfortunately, Harrison died shortly after taking office, leaving the dreaded John Tyler, a Virginia slaveholder, as president.[34]

The party made its best single showing in 1842, when Samuel Sewall received 5.4 percent of the vote for the Massachusetts governorship, running on the Liberty line, and thus threw the election into the State Legislature. The Liberty Party also held the balance of power in many Massachusetts elections in 1843 and 1844. In the latter year, Birney was again the party's presidential candidate. With better organization (and the candidate present in the country during the campaign this time), the party polled an improved, but disappointing, 62,000 votes (about 2.3 percent of votes cast). The most notable electoral outcome pertinent to the party was its *de facto* delivery of New York, and therefore the election, to James K. Polk, as most antislavery voters otherwise favored Henry Clay.[35] Though the major parties ignored the Liberty Party and the slavery issue in 1840, the growing Liberty Party presence and the issue of the annexation of Texas both drew greater attention to the cause.

Party fortunes ebbed after 1844, due to the aforementioned discouragement over the electoral outcomes, as well as to the escalating concern with other issues. But most importantly, a shift in antislavery politics occurred with the introduction and subsequent debate over the Wilmot Proviso, which attempted to bar the extension of slavery into any territories acquired from Mexico. The principle of limiting by statute the furtherance of slavery served as a key rallying point for antislavery forces, and it precipitated the rise of the Free Soil Party, the broader, more pragmatic successor to the Liberty Party.[36] The party's other key connection to subsequent antislavery efforts was that it was successful far beyond its numbers in spreading antislavery sentiment—mostly through public education efforts conducted via lectures, newspapers, pamphlets, and conventions.[37] The party's contribution to the antislavery movement and public debate was certainly more significant than the number of votes it received.

FREE SOIL PARTY

Built as it was from the electoral failures of the Liberty Party,[38] the Free Soil Party differed from its predecessor in a number of important respects. First, it was more diverse in its composition, especially as it included predominant numbers of disaffected Democrats and Whigs. Second, it expanded the scope of issues it addressed. Third, its attack on slavery was limited to the issue of containment raised in the Wilmot Proviso. Fourth, it emphasized economic and political concerns over moral ones, as contrasted with the Liberty Party. Fifth, it focused much more directly on vying with the major parties for the growing antislavery vote.

The establishment of the Free Soil Party was prompted most directly by a split in the New York State Democratic Party between the "Hunkers" (those who "hunkered" for office at the expense of principle), who turned a blind eye to the slavery issue, and the "Barnburners" (alluding to the Dutch farmer who burned his barn to get rid of the rats inside), who vigorously opposed slavery. The two factions split over the Wilmot Proviso, and each sent its own delegation to the national Democratic

Convention in Baltimore in 1848. After much dispute and in-
decision, the Barnburners withdrew, held their own convention
in Utica, New York, endorsed former president Martin Van
Buren, and announced their willingness to join with others behind a free soil platform. A similar split occurred within the
Whig Party. It, too, was polarized over the slavery issue between
antislavery "Conscience" Whigs and proslavery "Cotton"
Whigs. When the Whig convention nominated Virginia slaveholder Zachary Taylor, the Conscience Whigs pulled out.[39] The
third element of the new party included former Liberty Party
adherents.

Although political opportunism would seem to have been an
important motivating force behind the actions of these factions,
it is clear that they were impelled by both politics and principles.
A study of selected members of each of these three factions
found parallel sentiments. The Barnburners studied were
strongly opposed to the extension of slavery beyond its existing
domain, but also were concerned with political expediency
(seeking a way to inflict punishment on the Hunkers). The Conscience Whigs felt that, as a moral imperative, the federal government should do everything possible to separate itself from
slavery. The former Liberty men realized that the goals of free
soil were more modest, but also realized that the new party was
the only practical way to fight the evil of slavery.[40] Thus,
"[a]lthough the Free Soilers stressed ideology and sincerely believed in the anti-extension cause, they were also politicians
hungry for office and political power."[41]

The party itself was composed of two elements—the "pragmatics" and the "ideologues." The pragmatics viewed Free Soil
as a way station, or a device to apply leverage on the major
parties. Though bound to the party by a commitment to contain
slavery, "they usually acted instead like politicians in quest of
a job."[42] The ideologues were the idealists unerringly dedicated
to the free soil principle.[43]

As the description of the pragmatic element of the party implies, it was not at the leading edge of the antislavery movement.
Indeed, the Free Soil Party "was not an abolitionist organization
and resisted being identified as one."[44] As William Lloyd Garrison said of the party in 1848, "It is a party for keeping Free

Soil and not for setting men free."[45] In addition, a faction of the Liberty Party refused to join the Free Soilers, believing that they did not go far enough. This faction formed the Liberty League (supported by previous presidential candidate Birney) and ran Gerrit Smith for president in 1848; he drew 2,600 votes. Liberty men often spoke publicly against political and social discrimination; Free Soilers did not.[46]

In fact, much anti-black sentiment existed among members of the free soil movement. The Wilmot Proviso issue was itself a double-edged sword. While it attempted to block the further spread of slavery, it also served as a convenient means for keeping blacks in the South, and out of the territories. The Wilmot Proviso was justifiably referred to as the "White Man's Resolution."[47] Racism and white supremacy were also ingrained in the Free Soil Party.[48] At the same time, however, the Free Soilers promoted many racial reforms in northern states, fighting for blacks' right to vote, testify in court, attend school, and travel freely between the states. Thus, fighting institutional racism was also part of the Free Soil record.[49]

This large, diverse coalition came together in Buffalo, New York, in August, 1848. As many as 20,000 delegates and spectators jammed the enormous tent used for the convention. The convention itself was a mix of political excitement and religious fervor.[50] One analyst referred to the convention as having "a spontaneous, almost religious atmosphere."[51] More than anything else, descriptions of the convention resemble those of a religious revival meeting. Yet, the unity of principle and pragmatism was evident. "The Buffalo convention represented a peak in free soil enthusiasm and spirit, as dedication and opportunism combined to produce a highly meaningful political challenge."[52]

The keystone of the Free Soil platform was opposition to slavery extension. As such, it was the only party to endorse the Wilmot Proviso principle in 1848. (Democratic presidential candidate Lewis Cass believed that the territories should decide the slave issue for themselves; Whig candidate Taylor was silent on the issue.[53]) Hoping to broaden their appeal, Free Soil leaders were careful to include other issues in their platform. In addition to urging total federal government separation from slavery, they also advocated cheap postage, reduced federal spending, tariff reform, upgrading of rivers and harbors, and free homesteading. These planks were consciously and calculatingly added to appeal to as many voters as possible. They also wished to distance themselves from the Liberty Party's single-issue tunnel vision.[54] The most reluctant faction at the convention was that of the former Liberty Party members. Though politically less influential than some of the Barnburners and Conscience Whigs, their standing in the antislavery movement was important for the legitimacy it could bestow on the Free Soil cause. Liberty leaders thus exchanged their support (except for those who formed the Liberty League) for platform concessions. Yet these were modest. Missing from the Free Soil platform was any declaration of support for the principle of abolition (ending slavery where it then existed), any denunciation of the Fugitive Slave Act or the three-fifths clause in the Constitution (which counted five slaves as three citizens eligible for representation in the Congress). Nor was anything said about racial discrimination. Despite these lapses, most former Liberty men rallied readily to the Free Soil banner.[55]

The party's relative compromise on the slavery issue was also evidenced in its choice of presidential and vice-presidential nominees. Martin Van Buren had been the choice of the Barnburners, and their early endorsement of the New Yorker all but sealed the outcome. Yet Van Buren's antislavery credentials were less than sterling. While president, he was known as "the Northern man with Southern principles."[56] In 1844, he expressed his hostility to slavery expansion but continued to state his opposition to ending slavery in the District of Columbia. He did agree, however, to approve such a measure before accepting the nod in 1848.[57] The vice-presidential candidate, Charles Francis Adams, was a Conscience Whig as well as the son of one president and the grandson of another. Yet his antislavery credentials were also undistinguished. But without doubt, any misgivings about the candidates were more than offset by the enticing possibility that this new third party could truly challenge major-party hegemony.[58]

The election results were a disappointment. Van Buren received about 291,000 votes (10 percent of votes cast), with more than half of his vote coming from New York and Massachusetts. The ticket carried no states, but did carry three counties in New England, eight in the mid-Atlantic states, and 21 in the Midwest. Though drawing from both parties, the Free Soilers' effort probably hurt the Democrats more. They did succeed in electing 12 men to Congress who continued to represent the bulwark of the antislavery movement in succeeding years, and they held the balance of power in the Ohio State Legislature. Party totals were diminished by lack of organization and funds and by the preemption of the free soil issue by the major parties. Lewis Cass was a northerner who argued that popular sovereignty would have the effect of keeping the territories free; Zachary Taylor declared that he would sign the Wilmot Proviso. Perhaps most importantly, party loyalties among voters helped keep potential strays within the major-party flocks.[59] Still, the election served to legitimize the principles behind the Free Soil slogan, "Free Soil, Free Speech, Free Labor, and Free Men."

After the election, dissent erupted within the party. As the major parties had succeeded in co-opting the slave issue, most Free Soilers readily returned to their major-party homes. In exchange, the regular parties offered patronage and platform concessions on anti-extensionism. By 1852, the Free Soil Party consisted mostly of former Liberty men and Whigs.[60]

The final blow to the party was the Compromise of 1850. Adopted in that year, it admitted California as a free state, let Utah and New Mexico decide the issue for themselves, and abolished slave trade (though not slavery itself) in the nation's capital; however, it also strengthened the Fugitive Slave Act, giving the federal government more power to help slaveowners track down fugitive slaves, and it levied penalties on those who assisted fugitive slaves. Clearly, the compromise was at odds with free soil principles; yet the country was so anxious to seek a final solution to the slavery problem that it was embraced as such by most. Both major-party candidates for president in 1852 backed the compromise.[61]

The Free Soil Party met again in 1852, renaming itself Free Democrats. With the pragmatics mostly gone, the party closely resembled the Liberty Party of 1840.[62] In its platform, it announced continued commitment to the Wilmot Proviso and to the separation of the government from slavery, and it attacked the Compromise of 1850. It also avowed support for the principle of abolition, denouncing slavery as sinful. As in 1848, it endorsed free land, internal improvements, and cheap postage, and it extended welcome to new immigrants (a swipe at Know-Nothing nativism).[63]

The Free Democrats nominated a reluctant John P. Hale (a former Liberty man) for president. Despite the obvious handicaps, Hale received nearly 5 percent of the vote. Also, three Free Democrats were elected to Congress. Though this was the final year for the Free Soil movement, it was also the Whig Party's last election, foreshadowing the rise of the Republican Party and events leading up to the Civil War.

THE GREENBACK PARTY

The post–Civil War era saw the rise of numerous third parties and other political movements that were to have profound consequences for the electoral system of the latter part of the nineteenth century. As with political movements in all eras, economics played a key role in stimulating and motivating discontent.

During the Civil War, the government had expanded the money supply by printing paper currency ("greenbacks") as a means of financing wartime expenditures. After the war, the government contracted the money supply to eliminate the extra paper currency. This action resulted in falling prices and pervasive unemployment. Agriculture in particular was hard hit, and it continued to suffer from economic depression throughout the 1870s. Farmers sought policies to alleviate their distress. They organized to decrease the profits of middlemen (especially those involved in commodity transport, like the railroads), increase the price of products, and limit debts by increasing the money supply in circulation. "Currency inflation" in particular had been a perennial cause of farmers, especially during times of depression, since the Revolutionary War.[64]

One response to these persistent problems was the formation of Granges—semi-secret societies aimed at improving rural cultural and social life. Grange organizations coalesced in many states, attempting to promote railroad regulation, civil service, and banking and taxation reform, among other goals. Meeting with some initial successes, state-enacted reforms were often subsequently invalidated by the courts. Though the greenback cause—increasing the currency supply—was not initially the keystone of Grange organizations, these political efforts (including various state "Independent Parties" formed to influence the electoral process) helped to pave the way for the Greenback Party.[65]

The first concrete attempt to bring the greenback issue into party politics came not from farmers, however, but from Eastern labor. As early as 1868, the National Labor Union promoted the paper currency principle. In February, 1872 the National Labor Party convention adopted a greenback platform, nominating David Davis of Illinois as its presidential candidate. As these activities suggest, no clear-cut division between the major parties existed on the currency question.[66]

Farmers' economic woes intensified with the panic of 1873, and this further downturn prompted many farmers to embrace greenbackism as their preeminent political issue. Greenback sympathies appeared first in Indiana and Illinois. Drawing initially on the Grangers' Independent Party structures, a convention was held in Indianapolis in November, 1874. Seven states were represented, and it produced a platform which concluded that the greatest problem facing the country was "the proper solution of the money question."[67] The first full national convention was held the following year in Cleveland. Representatives from 12 states convened to complete the organization of the party, and they officially adopted the name of the Independent Party (though this is in fact what was also known then and now as the Greenback Party).

The rise of the Greenback Party was instrumental in publicizing and legitimizing the paper currency principle; yet it was only part of a large, decentralized and diverse political and social movement. In addition to the party, separate Greenback clubs sprang up in large numbers, mostly in the Northwest (over 4,000 by 1878).[68] The Granger movement and other farm protest groups continued to be politically active. Also, a significant wing of the Democratic Party shared sympathies with greenbackism.

Finally, Eastern labor (including the Knights of Labor) also promoted the paper money principle.[69] In short, a plethora of geographically and socially diverse grassroots groups and factions
comprised this movement.[70] The party's presidential nominating convention converged on
Indianapolis in May, 1876. About 240 delegates from 18 states
met to promote greenbackism in the presidential election. The
party produced a platform that was solely concerned with the
paper money issue. In particular, it railed against the Specie
Resumption Act, which mandated the removal of paper money
from circulation. The platform called contraction "suicidal and
destructive."[71] The convention's presidential nominee was 85–
year-old philanthropist Peter Cooper.

As with the movement as a whole, the convention was attended by a wide array of social types, including businessmen,
labor reform leaders, lawyers, politicians, and farm leaders. Yet
all these delegates were united by the common and strong bond
of greenbackism.[72] Many of the Greenback leaders were pragmatics who had no illusions about greenbackism as a panacea;
nevertheless, "to see the convention as an assemblage of economic pressure groups would be a mistake. At bottom it consisted of True Believers—greenback ideologues who had
converged on the movement from many directions."[73] The political mysticism surrounding greenbackism pervaded the party
and the movement. Indeed, it possessed "the quality of a trans-
figuring faith," even to the extent of exhibiting a "quasi-religious
nature."[74]

The 1876 campaign was a disappointment for the party. The
campaign itself was weak and poorly organized, hampered in
particular by a lack of funds. In fact, the nomination of Cooper
was prompted in large part by the hope that he would use his
personal wealth to bankroll the party, but he gave less than had
been hoped, and most of that went to educational literature.[75]
The party was also hurt by the encroaching Democrats. While
the Republicans generally ignored the greenback issue, many
greenback sympathizers remained within the Democratic Party
(despite a weak greenback plank in the Democratic platform),
who in turn reaped the political harvest planted by the non-
Democratic greenbackers. As a consequence, Democrats did well

in 1876. Cooper polled only about 82,000 votes (0.9 percent), and the Greenback Party could claim only a handful of seats in the Illinois State Legislature.[76]

Though the party was demoralized by the poor showing, it began to revive itself almost immediately. Numerous state party conventions were held in 1877; in subsequent state elections around the country, Greenback candidates polled 5–15 percent of the vote for various races.[77] This Greenback rally was attributable not only to revived organization but to a deepening agricultural depression.

As if to emphasize its grassroots nature, the Greenback Party reached its high-water mark in 1878. Despite the absence of a presidential contest that year, party candidates managed to accumulate a million votes nationwide. A key catalyst contributing to this electoral flurry was the party's 1878 convention in Toledo, as it brought together both farm and labor interests. About 1,100 delegates representing 28 states attended. In addition to reaffirming greenback principles, the party's platform also included labor-inspired proposals to limit the workday, create a government labor bureau, and restrict Chinese immigration. Nevertheless, the platform was still a greenback document, as it also called for an income tax, homesteading, and silver coinage.[78] Despite the changing nature of this revised greenback coalition, "the convention was dominated by the reformers and ideologues who had been active in greenback politics since the '60's."[79]

The Greenback Party registered successes across the country. In all, it elected fifteen representatives to Congress—six from the East, six from the Midwest, and three from the South. Of its million total votes, almost two-thirds came from the Midwest, and one-third from the South. Yet much of its success came from fusion with sympathetic Republicans in the South and Democrats in the rest of the country.[80] The question of whether to fuse with major-party elements or maintain the minor party's integrity would become ever more troublesome for party leaders.

This split emerged most clearly at the party's 1880 convention in Chicago. The anti-fusionists, known as the "radicals," supported by the Greenback clubs, resisted the fusion principle, fearing the loss of identity and autonomy. They pushed hardest for a separate presidential candidate, evincing their "hostility to any compromise or coalition with the Democrats."[81] The "fu-sionists" sought a union with Democrats as the most expeditious means to promoting greenbackism. The radicals attempted to preempt the fusionists by holding a convention in March, 1880 in St. Louis (three months before the scheduled party convention in Chicago), claiming to represent 10,000 Greenback clubs and 2,000,000 voters. Led by Marcus Pomeroy, the convention nominated Stephen D. Dillaye of New York for president; he declined the offer. The convention then adjourned, agreeing to reconvene at the very place and time of the full convention.[82] In Chicago, the radicals carried the day with the nomination of General James B. Weaver of Iowa, who himself created some history by becoming the first presidential candidate to aggressively stump the country. He reportedly traveled 20,000 miles, made 100 speeches, shook 30,000 hands, and was heard by 500,000 people.[83] The party's 1880 platform was the same as that of 1878, with the addition of planks for female suffrage and national regulation of interstate commerce.

Yet for all of this, Weaver garnered only about 3 percent of the vote (about 308,000 votes), with most of his support coming from the West. The party also elected 10 members to Congress. These disappointing results are attributable to two primary factors—fusionist ties to the major parties in many areas (helping the cause, but hurting the party apparatus), and generalized economic improvement. In particular, corn, wheat, and oats prices were more favorable that year.[84]

Disintegration set in after 1880. The intra-party struggle between the fusionists and radicals increased, but most pragmatic party members began drifting back to the major parties. The extent of the drift was such that, as a consequence, the Democrats did exceptionally well in the 1882 elections.[85] In that year, only one Greenbacker was elected to Congress.

The party held one more convention, at Indianapolis, in 1884, where it nominated the Anti-Monopoly Party's presidential candidate, General Benjamin F. Butler. The party's 1884 platform paralleled that of 1880. Despite hard campaigning, Butler received only about 175,000 votes (about half of Weaver's total). After the election, remaining members either fused with the Democrats or joined other minority factions.[86]

Although the Greenback Party rose and fell with economic trends, it was not simply a party of economics. As one observer noted,

Soft money and hard money were far more than congeries of economic interests. . . . They were also competing intellectual and ethical systems. On a moral plane, Agrarianism confronted Calvinism; on the intellectual, a revived mercantilism confronted the prevailing economic orthodoxy. In both cases the hard money position, reinforced by the prestige of the Protestant Churches and the academy respectively, enjoyed an immense advantage over the soft money ideology so often identified with quacks, visionaries and charlatans.[87]

The role of religious leaders was relatively marginal compared to their role in other single-issue parties examined here.[88] Still, an overriding moral imperative clearly motivated and fueled the greenback debate—and the party it engendered.

THE PROHIBITION PARTY

The crusade against alcohol has been one of American history's most enduring social/moral single-issue crusades. The persistence of this movement is epitomized in party politics by America's third oldest (and oldest third) party, the Prohibition Party. Although its historic consequences are relatively minor, the party is in many ways a prototype of past and present single-issue parties.

The Prohibition Party's antecedents extend back to several independently formed state parties of the 1850s, including the Temperance and Maine Law parties in Maine, New York's Anti-Dramshop Party, and Pennsylvania's Prohibition Party. The leaders of these grassroots parties were also involved with the abolition of slavery movement, and the birth of the Republican Party.[89]

The resolution of slavery at the conclusion of the Civil War prompted prohibitionists to turn their full attention to the temperance problem.[90] Despite early links with the Republicans, however, neither of the major parties proved receptive to the concerns of prohibitionists. As one Prohibition Party leader later observed, "the Republican Party had betrayed its original humanitarianism spirit in favor of business as usual."[91] The party's formation was also enhanced by the fact that many states repealed prohibition measures passed before the Civil War, and others had ceased enforcement. In addition, the liquor industry, including tavern owners, brewers and others, was acquiring political influence.[92] The resurgence of alcohol seemed to be embodied by the country's president (and reputed drinker), Ulysses S. Grant.

The first national party convention was held in Chicago in September, 1869. About 500 delegates representing 19 states attended. During the next three years, the party ran candidates for state and local offices in at least seven states. In 1872, the party met in Columbus, Ohio, to nominate its first candidates for nationwide office. A singular feature of the convention was the nomination of a variety of distinguished men for president, including Supreme Court Chief Justice Salmon Chase and several generals and former antislavery leaders. The convention settled on a lesser light, however—James Black, a stalwart prohibitionist who had also helped found the Republican Party in the 1850s.[93] The close moral connection between temperance and the abolition of slavery was evidenced in the initial overlap in the leadership of both movements. As the 1872 convention keynote speaker observed, "Slavery is gone . . . but drunkenness stays."[94]

The electoral consequences of this first effort were minuscule—Black received a paltry 5,607 votes[95]—but this and subsequent conventions were significant for the reforms they advocated that ultimately became national policy. The 1869 convention advocated universal women's suffrage, civil service reform, and direct election of senators. Subsequent conventions advocated inheritance and income tax legislation, child labor regulations, and pensions for the elderly. The party's attention to issue/ideological concerns as reflected in its platforms prompted one party analyst to observe, with some sarcasm, that the 1872 platform in particular "was so verbose that only a few newspapers printed excerpts from it while most ignored it entirely."[96] The party's principal issue concern was, of course, prohibition. Ironically, however, analysts agree that the party had nothing to do with, and could claim no credit for, the passage of the Eighteenth Amendment.[97]

The Prohibition Party's fortunes improved modestly in subsequent elections, reaching a high water mark of 271,000 votes (2.25 percent of presidential votes cast) in 1892. Though the party's vote did not fluctuate wildly over time, its ideological predilections did. The party's history can, in fact, be divided into three periods, according to the ascension of either "narrow-gaugers," who stressed adherence to the prohibition issue alone, or "broad-gaugers," who wished the party to broaden its issue concerns and adopt a more pragmatic political approach.[98] The struggle between these two factions marked most of the party's history.

The first period, from the party's founding until 1896, was delineated by the dominance of the broad-gaugers. This was reflected in the diversity of issue positions addressed in most of the party platforms during this time, as well as by various attempts to merge or join forces with the growing Populist Party. Many prohibitionists viewed the populist movement with great satisfaction and anticipation, as both movements shared similar constituencies and perspectives. Most Populist Party leaders endorsed prohibition in some form, as well as women's suffrage (though the latter to a lesser degree).[99] Despite attempts at fusion in many states in the early 1890s, however, the effort ultimately failed because of the populists' refusal to accept an uncompromising prohibition plank.

If flirtations with the Populist Party did not result in an enduring union, the fusion issue did help to bring to a head the ongoing dispute between narrow- and broad-gaugers. At the party's 1896 convention, the narrow-gaugers succeeded in asserting their perspective by eliminating other issues, except for female suffrage, from the party's platform. This occurred despite considerable evidence that most party leaders favored the broader approach.[100] The success of the narrow-gauge faction ruptured the convention. Many broad-gaugers left the party to join the Democrats, or drop out of politics. Others formed their own competing party, the National Party, which reflected the broad-gauge approach (it was also known as the Free Silver

Prohibition Party).[101] Not surprisingly, the Prohibition Party garnered less than half of its 1892 vote in the pivotal 1896 election
(130,000 votes). The Nationals received fewer than 14,000 votes.
The ascension of the narrow-gaugers in 1896 marked the beginning of the party's second period, characterized not only by
sole concern with the single issue of prohibition, but also by the
beginning of a turn to the right that became fully evident by
1912.[102] Progressive influences lingered, though, because of the
influence of the Progressive Party in the first decade of the twentieth century.[103]

The Prohibition Party would never recover from the 1896 election: as the party's "sense of failure became more and more
acute, Prohibitionists drew further away from the commitment
to social change which had marked their party before 1896."[104]
Yet, electoral setbacks did not diminish the ideological fervor of
the remaining party adherents. In fact, despite the party's drub-
bing, its National Executive Committee issued a manifesto—
three weeks after the election—that warned against deviating
from or otherwise compromising on the prohibition issue. It also
warned about any future attempts to fuse with other parties.[105]

During this second period, national attention to prohibition
shifted away from the party, and toward axe-wielding Carry
Nation, the Women's Christian Temperance Union (WCTU) and
the Anti-Saloon League (ASL). The ASL was especially important because it demonstrated that citizens could be politically
effective without leaving one of the major parties. This fact flew
directly in the faces of Prohibition Party leaders, which lent fuel
to the resentment and petulance felt towards the WCTU and
especially the ASL.[106] If organizational jealousy helped spark this
intra-movement feuding, so too did the fears of party leaders
that the Prohibition Party might wind up being subsumed by
the ASL if it cooperated too freely. Party leaders openly attacked
the ASL and expressed ambivalence about the work of Carry
Nation.[107] In the sparring that continued between the elements
of the prohibition movement, the principal loser was the party.[108]
The great political success of the prohibition movement was the
passage of the prohibition amendment to the Constitution in
1919. Responsibility for this feat lies clearly with the ASL, which
itself is a classic example of pressure politics at work. One analyst

went so far as to conclude that the ASL was "the most effective pressure group in American political history."[109]

During the reign of prohibition in the 1920s, the party occupied itself by working against political candidates and officeholders who shared "wet" sentiments, and also by pushing for firmer administration of prohibition.[110]

In 1928, the party departed from its longstanding position that no differences between the major parties existed, by endorsing Herbert Hoover. The party still ran its own candidate but promised not to run in areas where Hoover might be hurt. It even promised to withdraw entirely if such a move was necessary to Hoover's victory.[111]

The final stage of the party's evolution, from 1932 to the present, marks the return to the prohibition crusade with the repeal of the Eighteenth Amendment in 1933. This final period has also been characterized by movement toward "elitist, conservative reform."[112] By the 1950s, the party had "built an appeal based on distrust of government, calling for decentralization, states' rights, limited taxation, and an end to restraints on free enterprise."[113] Party control thus reverted back to those with multi-issue concerns. Efforts to signal the party's broader interests were reflected in the party's name change in the 1976 and 1980 elections to the New Statesman Party, though the consequent voter confusion prompted a return to the original name.[114]

Today's Prohibition Party is identified by the "intense nationalism, economic conservatism, and social stagnation of the radical right."[115] The 1980 platform called, for example, for a return to the gold standard, a balanced federal budget, federal regulation reduction, and less court interference in national policy, as well as a condemnation of the "sellout" of nationalist China and the "giveaway" of the Panama Canal.[116]

Having sketched out the essentials of the Prohibition Party's history, we now turn to a consideration of the motivational bases that propelled adherents' involvement in a party where the prospects for electoral success—a prime motivator for electoral participation—have been virtually nonexistent, even in the party's heyday.

Without doubt, the political fires that kept party members warm during many cold years were the moralistic, single-minded, uncompromising, zealous convictions of party adherents. The prior activities of party founders and early adherents reveal close ties to the antislavery movement (clearly a movement sharing striking motivational similarities), as well as a heavily religious cast of its membership.[117] Party platforms expressed a consistent concern for societal decline in morality, and the necessity for actions to bring about a "spiritual awakening."[118]

Today, the adverse consequences of excessive alcohol consumption not only are well-known but also are directly related to recent policy changes, such as the national effort to raise the legal drinking age to 21. Yet the moral fervor surrounding this issue in the nineteenth and early twentieth centuries seems quaint, in retrospect. It was , however, anything but quaint to activists of the time.

For the prohibitionist of years gone by, sobriety was far more than the absence of alcohol: "The virtue which he [the prohibitionist] felt must lie in sobriety was demonstrated not merely by conformity to the laws of God . . . but also by the unmistakable authority of worldly success."[119] The Prohibition Party's cause was not just a political issue; it was, in fact, virtually a prerequisite for entrance into Heaven. Thus, the concerns of politics, as well as salvation, became inextricably intertwined, as for example when party Chairman Samuel Dickie observed in 1888 that all eight of the party's previous presidential and vice-presidential candidates were still alive, whereas only four of sixteen major-party candidates survived. Dickie told his party convention that this fact clearly illustrated "God's Providence."[120]

Compared with other elements of the movement, the Prohibition Party pursued the greatest degree of issue purity, avoidance of compromise, and zealotry. This was evidenced not only by its lack of growth despite the widespread appeal of the temperance issue, but also by its attack on the Christian church. Especially in the latter part of the nineteenth century, the party asserted that "a Christian lacking commitment to prohibition was no Christian at all."[121] The measuring stick for a Christian's devotion to temperance became support for the party, since neither major party was adequately strong on the issue. To support either major party was to support, even if indirectly, demon rum. Since alcohol was the devil's work, so too were the major parties. One party leader observed, "It is not Christian to vote for rum directly or indirectly. Christian men can't do it and maintain their Christian standing."[122] This attitude led to the logical, if politically suicidal, demand that major-party voters be expelled from the churches for supporting parties that tolerated the liquor interests.[123] The consequences of this political approach were symbolized in microcosm when in 1902 a Wisconsin party organizer called on a prohibitionist, only to find him lying drunk in the snow in the middle of the road. As the organizer said later, "We helped him in the house, and went on our way sorrowing."[124]

Given political tactics seemingly designed to alienate most potential supporters, the ascendance of the ASL followed logically. The League succeeded where the party failed, by employing tactics precisely opposite those of the party. In particular, it labored to work through the major parties, in cooperation with (and relying on support from) the churches, and it adopted a more pragmatic, less zealous, ideological approach that "would disturb, outside of the liquor industry, none of the institutional arrangements of American society."[125]

The pattern of the Prohibition Party, even when in the hands of the broad-gaugers, reflects the kind of single-issue intensity that casts aside what most Americans would consider politics as usual. At the same time, this tunnel vision dooms the party to relative electoral obscurity. Yet even the Prohibition Party could make some claim to influencing politics, as least in its heyday. It did anticipate policy changes that would evolve in areas such as women's rights, the income tax, and prohibition. These issues later appeared in the major party platforms. It succeeded, especially in its early years, in promoting more stringent legislation at the state and local levels, pertaining to the sale and consumption of alcohol, as well as in teaching about the effects of alcohol. It also helped push Congress to adopt in 1886 an alcohol instruction law for the District of Columbia and federal territories, which represented the first national temperance measure passed in 52 years.[126] Though these achievements seem minor, they nevertheless remind us that minor parties can and do play an interactive role in the larger political and policy process.

SUMMARY

The four cases of single-issue parties examined here reveal remarkable similarities. Each party possessed within itself an enduring bi-factional split between those seeking issue purity (and also disdaining union with outside elements who lacked similar purity) and those who sought a broader, more pragmatic political approach. The latter "broad" factions felt the pull to seek relative moderation and conciliation to enhance the party's base and legitimacy. The "narrow" factions held issue purity and homogeneity above more mundane political concerns.

Each party was also part of a larger social movement. Without exception, single-issue parties were symptomatic of broader and deeper issue concerns not adequately addressed by the major parties or other mechanisms of popular expression. In two of the four cases (Liberty and Prohibition), the parties were the most extreme and zealous parts of the larger movement (for the Liberty Party, this was true within the antislavery movement; it was not a part of the abolitionist movement, which generally abhorred action within the existing political framework). Within the Greenback Party, a portion of party supporters, led by Marcus Pomeroy, embodied the most extreme element of the party. But this faction's control over the party was limited, based mostly in separate Greenback clubs (though this faction did well within the party from 1880 on). The Free Soil Party also included in it some of the more radical elements of the antislavery movement, but its more pragmatic objectives (as a reaction to the failure of the Liberty Party, and the apparent electability of Van Buren) clearly steered it in a more moderate direction, despite standing alone on the Wilmot Proviso issue. The Liberty Party, on the other hand, stood in the undisputed forefront of the antislavery movement. It was ideologically outflanked by Garrison and the abolitionists, but abolitionism was itself a separate movement from the antislavery movement, as mentioned.

The most cursory examination of the four parties clearly highlighted the preeminence of issue concerns, even in the case of the relatively pragmatic Free Soil Party. This follows naturally from the force of single issues as the critical coalescing agents. In accordance with issue preeminence, political education was also a key goal. Generally speaking, both of these concerns dwarfed the usual party goal of seeking and achieving elective office.

The potency of certain single issues also suggests close association with substantial grassroots activism. Each single-issue party was built and sustained from the bottom up, owing precisely to the potency of the pertinent issue. Grassroots support is certainly common to American parties; yet none demonstrate greater dependence on the grassroots than single-issue parties.

Consistent with issue preeminence, all of the single-issue parties raised issues that touched highly sensitive nerves in at least some significant segments of the body politic. The unwillingness or inability of the major parties to address these issues underscores both the issues' potency and the shortcomings of the major parties at various times in history. Minor parties thus serve both as gauge and as safety valve; they indicate the presence of important, usually unaddressed concerns, and they provide an intra-system outlet for cumulating political pressure.

The salience of these issues is logically connected, in two of the four cases, to Constitution-related remedies. That is, the parties either sought a change in the Constitution or a remedy with constitutional consequences.

The final two characteristics listed in Table 1.1 speak to the nature of the issues giving rise to these parties. Without question, all of the issues involved (slavery, prohibition, paper currency) provoked emotions far beyond those associated with most conventional political concerns. Two of these issues, slavery and prohibition, clearly fall within the realm of "social regulation."[127] The traits associated with this category of issues include highly ideological conflict and the presence of single-issue groups. In fact, single-issue groups are identified as playing a crucial role in connecting grassroots activism with the governmental process. The nature of political conflict surrounding social regulation is polarized and intense, and marked by an unwillingness to compromise or negotiate.[128] In addition, the very definition of social regulatory policy is that it involves "the use of authority to modify or replace social values, institutional practices, and norms of interpersonal behavior with new modes of conduct based upon legal prescriptions."[129] Thus, these issues are framed

Table 1.1
Salient Characteristics Shared by Single-Issue Parties

PARTY	Intra-party bi-factionalism: narrow vs. broad	Is party part of broader social movement?	Is party regarded as most zealous (extreme) element of movement?	Pre-eminence of issue purity over electoral success?	Is education of public a primary party objective?	Is party grassroots in origin and political strength?	Party succeed in introducing new salient issue(s)?	Constitution-related remedies/changes sought?	Religious leaders integral to movement?	Is issue framed in moral terms?
Liberty	"diehards" vs. "coalitionists"	yes	yes	yes	yes	yes	yes	yes	yes	yes
Free Soil	"ideologues" vs. "pragmatics"	yes	no	yes	yes	yes	yes	no	yes	yes
Prohibition	"narrow-gaugers" vs. "broad-gaugers"	yes	yes	yes	yes	yes	yes	yes	yes	yes
Greenback	"radicals" vs. "fusionists"	yes	no	yes	yes	yes	yes	no	no	yes

in moral terms and logically tend to include religious leaders among party leadership and followers. The only issue that did not follow this pattern among those considered here is greenbackism. Yet even though the question it raised was ostensibly one of economics, the emotive, moral fervor of the greenback movement set it apart from other economic concerns, nearer to classic "social regulation." As Table 1.1 shows, the Greenback Party shared fewer of the ascribed characteristics (seven out of ten) than any of the other parties. Nevertheless, the similarities outnumber and outweigh the differences.

The succeeding chapters will turn attention to the principal concern of this work—the modern-day single-issue Right to Life Party. After examining this party in far greater detail in the next two chapters, and then drawing back to consider some consequences of multi-partyism in Chapter 4, the final chapter will draw comparisons and offer some judgments.

NOTES

1. Steven J. Rosenstone, Roy L. Behr, and Edward Lazarus, *Third Parties in America* (Princeton, NJ: Princeton University Press, 1984), p. 80.
2. William B. Hesseltine, *Third Party Movements in the United States* (New York: Van Nostrand, 1962), p. 32.
3. For example, see Richard H. Sewell, *Ballots for Freedom* (New York: Oxford University Press, 1976), Ch. 3; Howard P. Nash, *Third Parties in American Politics* (Washington, DC: Public Affairs Press, 1959), p. 26.
4. Joseph G. Rayback, *Free Soil: The Election of 1848* (Lexington, KY: University of Kentucky Press, 1970), p. 56.
5. Sewell, *Ballots for Freedom*, p. 56.
6. Ibid., pp. 58–59.
7. Ibid., pp. 62, 72.
8. As stated, for example, in Rosenstone, Behr, and Lazarus, *Third Parties in America*, p. 49.
9. Sewell, *Ballots for Freedom*, pp. 43–47.
10. Nash, *Third Parties in American Politics*, p. 32.
11. Rayback, *Free Soil*, p. 57.
12. Sewell, *Ballots for Freedom*, pp. 90–91.
13. Ibid., p. 95.

14. Rayback, *Free Soil*, p. 106.

15. Sewell, *Ballots for Freedom*, pp. 80–81.

16. Rayback, *Free Soil*, p. 104.

17. Sewell, *Ballots for Freedom*, p. 66; see also pp. 44, 52, 54–55.

18. Ibid., p. 82.

19. Merton L. Dillon, *The Abolitionists* (DeKalb, IL: Northern Illinois University Press, 1974), p. 159.

20. Hesseltine, *Third Party Movements in the United States*, p. 32.

21. See, for example, Richard Hofstedter, *The Idea of a Party System* (Berkeley, CA: University of California Press, 1955); Austin Ranney, *Curing the Mischiefs of Faction* (Berkeley, CA: University of California Press, 1975), esp. Ch. 2.

22. Sewell, *Ballots for Freedom*, pp. 62, 67.

23. Ibid., pp. 101–6; Dillon, *The Abolitionists*, pp. 141–45.

24. Rayback, *Free Soil*, p. 99.

25. Hesseltine, *Third Party Movements in the United States*, pp. 33–34.

26. Rayback, *Free Soil*, pp. 43–47; see also Sewell, *Ballots for Freedom*, pp. 69, 74–76, 111; and Dillon, *The Abolitionists*, p. 146.

27. Sewell, *Ballots for Freedom*, p. 133.

28. Hesseltine, *Third Party Movements in the United States*, pp. 34–35.

29. Sewell, *Ballots for Freedom*, pp. 88–90.

30. Hesseltine, *Third Party Movements in the United States*, p. 35.

31. Sewell, *Ballots for Freedom*, pp. 116–117; see also Rayback, *Free Soil*, pp. 107–8.

32. Hesseltine, *Third Party Movements in the United States*, p. 34.

33. Rayback, *Free Soil*, pp. 104–6; see also Nash, *Third Party in American Politics*, p. 33.

34. Sewell, *Ballots for Freedom*, pp. 77–78.

35. Frederick Blue, *The Free Soilers* (Urbana, IL: University of Illinois Press, 1973), p. 7.

36. Hesseltine, *Third Party Movements in the United States*, p. 39.

37. Sewell, *Ballots for Freedom*, pp. 87–88, 164–65.

38. See, for example, ibid., p. 113; Blue, *The Free Soilers*, p. 7.

39. Hesseltine, *Third Party Movements in the United States*, pp. 39–40.

40. See Blue, *The Free Soilers*, Ch. 4.

41. Ibid., p. 151.

42. Ibid., p. x.

43. Ibid.

44. Dillon, *The Abolitionists*, p. 167.

45. Hesseltine, *Third Party Movements in the United States*, p. 42.
46. Blue, *The Free Soilers*, pp. 118–19, 107.
47. Sewell, *Ballots for Freedom*, p. 173.
48. Ibid., pp. 171–72; Blue, *The Free Soilers*, pp. 81, 87, 102, 290.
49. See Sewell, *Ballots for Freedom*, Ch. 8.
50. Nash, *Third Parties in American Politics*, p. 44.
51. Blue, *The Free Soilers*, p. 70.
52. Ibid., p. 80.
53. Ibid., pp. 121–22.
54. Sewell, *Ballots for Freedom*, p. 156; Blue, *The Free Soilers*, pp. 126–31.
55. Sewell, *Ballots for Freedom*, pp. 158–59.
56. Ibid., p. 153.
57. Ibid., pp. 153–54.
58. Ibid., p. 160.
59. Blue, *The Free Soilers*, pp. 110–13, 144; Sewell, *Ballots for Freedom*, p. 167.
60. Rosenstone, Behr, and Lazarus, *Third Parties in America*, pp. 54–55; Blue, *The Free Soilers*, p. 175; Sewell, *Ballots for Freedom*, pp. 226–28.
61. Rosenstone, Behr, and Lazarus, *Third Parties in America*, p. 55; Blue, *The Free Soilers*, pp. 178–79.
62. Hesseltine, *Third Party Movements in the United States*, p. 45.
63. Rosenstone, Behr, and Lazarus, *Third Parties in America*, p. 54; Blue, *The Free Soilers*, pp. 247–65; Sewell, *Ballots for Freedom*, pp. 244–46.
64. Solon J. Buck, *The Agrarian Crusade* (New Haven, CT: Yale University Press, 1921), pp. 77–80.
65. Hesseltine, *Third Party Movements in the United States*, pp. 51–52.
66. Buck, *The Agrarian Crusade*, pp. 79–80. See also Fred E. Haynes, *Third Party Movements Since the Civil War with Special Reference to Iowa* (Iowa City, IA: State Historical Society, 1916), pp. 124–25.
67. Buck, *The Agrarian Crusade*, pp. 81–82.
68. A classic work on farm-labor coalitions is Nathan Fine, *Labor and Farmer Parties in the United States: 1828–1928* (New York: Rand School of Social Science, 1928).
69. Haynes, *Third Party Movements*, pp. 116–19; 125–30.
70. Fine, *Labor and Farmer Parties*, p. 63.
71. Buck, *The Agrarian Crusade*, pp. 82–83.
72. Irwin Unger, *The Greenback Era: A Social and Political History of American Finance, 1865–1879* (Princeton, NJ: Princeton University Press, 1964), p. 306.

73. Ibid.

74. Ibid.

75. Ibid., p. 312.

76. Ibid., pp. 303, 308–10, 316–17; Buck, *The Agrarian Crusade*, pp. 85–86.

77. Hesseltine, *Third Party Movements in the United States*, p. 52; Unger, *The Greenback Era*, p. 327.

78. Hesseltine, *Third Party Movements in the United States*, pp. 52–53. Fine said the party platform was "a greenbacker's bible." *Labor and Farmer Parties*, p. 67.

79. Unger, *The Greenback Era*, p. 377.

80. Buck, *The Agrarian Crusade*, pp. 88–91; Unger, *The Greenback Era*, pp. 376–95; Fine, *Labor and Farmer Parties*, pp. 64–65.

81. Haynes, *Third Party Movements*, p. 136; Buck, *The Agrarian Crusade*, pp. 93–94.

82. Buck, *The Agrarian Crusade*, pp. 93–94.

83. Buck, *The Agrarian Crusade*, p. 94; Hesseltine, *Third Party Movements in the United States*, p. 54.

84. Buck, *The Agrarian Crusade*, pp. 95–96.

85. Haynes, *Third Party Movements*, pp. 144, 190–91, and Ch. 13. Fusion tactics swept the South. See Hesseltine, *Third Party Movements in the United States*, p. 53.

86. Fine, *Labor and Farmer Parties*, p. 71.

87. Unger, *The Greenback Era*, p. 404.

88. See Haynes, *Third Party Movements*, for examples of religious leaders involved with the movement; e.g., p. 132.

89. Roger C. Storms, *Partisan Prophets: A History of the Prohibition Party, 1854–1972* (Denver: National Prohibition Foundation, 1972), Ch. 1.

90. David L. Colvin, *Prohibition in the United States: A History of the Prohibition Party, and of the Prohibition Movement* (New York: Doran, 1926), p. 59.

91. Storms, *Partisan Prophets*, p. 4.

92. Rosenstone, Behr, and Lazarus, *Third Parties in America*, p. 76.

93. Norman Clark, *Deliver Us from Evil: An Interpretation of American Prohibition* (New York: W. W. Norton, 1976), p. 70.

94. Ibid.

95. All Prohibition Party vote totals through 1972 are taken from Storms, *Partisan Prophets*, Appendix A.

96. Nash, *Third Parties in American Politics*, p. 146. See also Frank Smallwood, *The Other Candidates* (Hanover, NH: University Press of New England, 1983), p. 37.

97. For example, see Nash, *Third Parties in American Politics*, p. 146; Jack S. Blocker, Jr., *Retreat from Reform: The Prohibition Movement in the United States, 1880–1913* (Westport, CT: Greenwood Press, 1976), pp. 155, 188, passim.

98. Ibid., pp. 70–71.

99. Ibid., p. 50.

100. Ibid., pp. 106–9.

101. Storms, *Partisan Prophets*, p. 23.

102. Blocker, *Retreat from Reform*, p. 226.

103. James H. Timberlake, *Prohibition and the Progressive Movement* (Cambridge: Harvard University Press, 1963), p. 34.

104. Blocker, *Retreat from Reform*, p. 188.

105. Ibid., p. 120.

106. One former party leader who jumped to the ASL condemned the party for its "bigotry, fanaticism, and narrowmindedness." Ibid., p. 142.

107. Ibid., p. 136–47.

108. Timberlake, *Prohibition and the Progressive Movement*, p. 157.

109. Clark, *Deliver Us from Evil*, p. 93; see also Timberlake, *Prohibition and the Progressive Movement*, Ch. 5.

110. Colvin, *Prohibition in the United States*, Ch. 24.

111. Joseph R. Gusfield, *Symbolic Crusade* (Urbana, IL: University of Illinois Press, 1963), p. 156.

112. Blocker, *Retreat from Reform*, p. 190.

113. Gusfield, *Symbolic Crusade*, p. 153.

114. Smallwood, *The Other Candidates*, p. 32.

115. Gusfield, *Symbolic Crusade*, p. 10.

116. Smallwood, *The Other Candidates*, pp. 37–38.

117. Blocker, *Retreat from Reform*, pp. 82–83.

118. Gusfield, *Symbolic Crusade*, p. 151.

119. Blocker, *Retreat from Reform*, p. 16.

120. Ibid., p. 17.

121. Ibid., p. 131.

122. Ibid., p. 132.

123. Ibid., p. 87.

124. Ibid., p. 127.

125. Ibid., p. 155. "... the [Anti-Saloon] League bureaucratized the prohibition impulse, striving to bend government to its will in response to the party's failure to organize a mass constituency capable of capturing the reins of power." Ibid., p. 210.

126. Colvin, *Prohibition in the United States*, Ch. 10.

127. See Raymond Tatalovich and Byron W. Daynes, "Moral Con-

troversies and the Policymaking Process," *Policy Studies Review* (February, 1984), esp. p. 205; also, Robert J. Spitzer, "Gun Control and the Mythology of the Second Amendment," in *The Social Agenda: Political Conflict and Public Policy*, ed. by Raymond Tatalovich and Byron W. Daynes, forthcoming.

128. Tatalovich and Daynes, "Moral Controversies and the Policy-making Process," p. 205.

129. Ibid.

2

A PARTY IS BORN: ABORTION AND THE RIGHT TO LIFE PARTY

Few would dispute the assertion that abortion has been the great social issue of the 1970s and 1980s. *Time* called abortion "the most emotional issue of politics and morality that faces the nation today."[1] Pollster Peter Hart concluded in the late 1970s that a quarter of American voters would vote against an incumbent solely on his/her abortion stand.[2] Conover and Gray found that single-issue voting for the issue of abortion was more potent than that for other issues studied, including busing, gun control, school prayer, and the Equal Rights Amendment.[3] As many as one-third of respondents measured in various polls indicated a willingness to vote on abortion alone (adding together supporters of both sides of the issue).[4] What sets the abortion issue apart from other potent social issues is its ability to arouse strong political passions among widespread groups in the electorate, especially on the right-to-life side. (In particular, Conover and Gray found much more one-issue behavior on the right-to-life than the pro-choice side.)[5] In this respect, it is a true grassroots movement.

ABORTION IN NEW YORK

Ever since New York became one of the first states in the nation to liberalize its abortion laws (predating the 1973 Supreme Court decision in *Roe v. Wade* by three years), the state's abortion practices have been subject to abundant public debate and political controversy. The reform law passed by the State Legislature in 1970 exceeded liberalized laws passed in 13 other states in the previous three years by eliminating restrictions on abortions during the first 24 weeks of pregnancy. New York was also the only state that did not require state residence as a prerequisite for obtaining an abortion, and it has been one of nine states to continue Medicaid funding of abortions for poor women since 1976, when Congress prohibited such use of federal funds with the passage of the Hyde Amendment. In 1977, about 25 percent of all state abortions were financed with state Medicaid dollars.[6]

New York has, not surprisingly, led the nation in numbers of abortions performed. From 1970 to 1979, state residents obtained about 1,342,000 abortions. Out-of-state residents obtained about 587,000 abortions in New York during this same period (though the annual number has declined steadily since 1972).[7] Census Bureau data records that, as of 1983, New York leads the other states with 731 abortions for every 1,000 live births.[8]

This thumbnail sketch of New York's abortion practices would seem to imply that state residents and political leaders have fairly uniform pro-choice attitudes; yet, such is not the case. In fact, the issue of abortion has, if anything, engendered more political upheaval in New York than in most states. The state legislature's consideration of a liberalized law in 1969 and 1970 prompted as much controversy and acrimonious debate as any issue in the legislature's history. Indeed, the legislature voted in 1972 to repeal the 1970 abortion law, only to have the measure vetoed by Governor Rockefeller. The very focus of this study, the Right to Life Party, represents a sharp partisan response to, and evidence of, the continuing swirl of controversy in state politics over this issue.

The attitudes of New Yorkers toward abortion seem, in fact, to reflect those of the country as a whole. A telephone survey of 804 New York residents conducted in 1980 revealed that 36 percent favored allowing a woman to seek an abortion under all circumstances, 55 percent favored allowing abortions under some circumstances, and 9 percent felt abortion should not be legal under any circumstances. A nationwide survey conducted by the National Opinion Research Center (NORC) at about the same time produced comparable response ratios to the same questions (41, 52 and 7 percent, respectively).[9]

If the differences between New Yorkers and the rest of the country are relatively minor, what then is it about New York that has engendered an anti-abortion political party? The answer is found in some unique characteristics of New York's political system that will be the focus of much attention here.

In particular, it is precisely New York's social and institutional context that has spawned a statewide single-issue party devoted solely to the abolition of abortion practices. The explanation for the existence of this party lies (aside from the omnipresence of the abortion issue itself) in the unique nature of New York's multi-party system.

NEW YORK'S ELECTORAL STRUCTURE

A full appreciation of the consequences of New York's electoral system begins with the initial establishment of a party. According to state election law, a political party may establish an automatic ballot line for all New York elections by fielding a candidate for governor who receives at least 50,000 votes in the general election.[10] If this threshold is reached, the party is guaranteed a ballot position in all New York elections for the next four years (until the next gubernatorial election). If no automatic ballot slot exists for a party or candidate, an individual seeking statewide office must obtain at least 20,000 petition signatures (signature requirements are less for non-statewide offices). Any registered voter may sign an independent candidate's petition, regardless of the voter's party affiliation, unless the voter has already signed a competing candidate's petition. In comparison with ballot-access requirements in other states, New York's is one of the most demanding. Despite this fact, determined and organized third parties can endure in New York where they cannot in other states, by virtue of another characteristic of state law.

Once a party does gain automatic ballot access, it must work to keep that slot and enhance the party's influence. The key provision of New York election law that helps the minor parties is the cross-endorsement rule. It says that parties may nominate candidates already endorsed by other parties. The votes a candidate receives on all his/her lines are then added together in the final count to determine the winner. Only two other states have this provision—Vermont and Connecticut. But in Vermont, the typical lack of close party competition between the major parties precludes the likelihood of minor parties providing the margin of difference. Connecticut possesses a high minimum in gubernatorial races (20 percent of the vote) as a requirement for party recognition.

The cross-endorsement system has a number of consequences for the New York party system, the sum total of which cause New York to resemble, in certain respects, European multi-party systems. First, this provision removes a major impediment to the casting of votes for minor parties—that is, the "wasted vote" syndrome. Voters frequently have preferences for third-party candidates but refrain from voting for them because of the feeling that they are throwing away their votes on a candidate or party that cannot win. But according to the cross-endorsement rule, votes cast for a candidate anywhere on the ballot are added to the candidate's total.

Second, one can easily calculate how many votes a party contributes to a candidate by observing the vote count on each line. Many quickly point out that a candidate would receive about the same total number of votes whether he/she appeared on one line or several, but candidates perceive that every line helps, especially in this politically competitive state. And who is to say that minor parties make no contribution under any circumstances? Evidence of the importance candidates attach to multiple party endorsements can be seen in their frequency. In 1978, for example, 145 of 210 state legislators had more than one ballot-line endorsement.

Third, minor parties may go beyond merely offering an additional line by offering the *only* line for a candidate denied a major-party line.While not a common occurrence, there have been instances of major-party candidates denied a major line who have gone on to win election on a minor-party line. In 1969, then-incumbent Republican New York Mayor John Lindsay was defeated in the Republican primary by John Marchi. Lindsay was nevertheless reelected by running on the Liberal Party line. It was later said that no Liberal Party activist seeking a municipal job went without work. In 1970, the Conservative Party succeeded in electing one of its own, James Buckley, to the U.S. Senate in a three-way race against the Democratic nominee, Richard Ottinger, and a liberal anti-Nixon Republican, Charles Goodell.

Fourth, minor parties can run their own candidates, or endorse others, to punish major-party candidates by depriving them of votes. In 1966, the Liberal Party ran the popular Franklin D. Roosevelt, Jr., for governor instead of endorsing the Democratic candidate, Frank O'Connor. Incumbent Nelson Rockefeller was viewed as being vulnerable to defeat that year, and the over half-million votes garnered by Roosevelt deprived O'Connor of the election (he lost by 392,000 votes). Alex Rose, then the leader of the Liberal Party, commented later that the move to nominate someone other than the Democratic nominee was sparked at least partly by a desire for retribution against Democratic leaders who were so sure of victory with or without Liberal support that they brushed aside attempts by Rose to have input in the process of nominating the Democratic candidate.[11]

Finally, minor parties can nominate candidates before the major parties do, to influence the choices of the major parties. Recent New York politics are replete with examples. In 1982, the Liberal party moved early to nominate Mario Cuomo for governor. Many felt that this influenced the subsequent Democratic primary between Cuomo and New York Mayor Ed Koch in Cuomo's favor because Democrats feared that if Cuomo lost the Democratic primary, his name would still appear on the November ballot, and as a result Democratic-Liberal votes would be split, as they had been in 1966, and thus allow Republican Lewis Lehrman to be elected. In 1980, an unknown town supervisor from Hempstead, Long Island, Alphonse D'Amato, got a critical early boost in his campaign for the U.S. Senate by receiving the nomination of the Conservative Party. He then went on to defeat incumbent Jacob Javits in the Republican primary and win election in November.

Major-party anxiety over this "tail wags dog" syndrome has

recently led leaders of both major parties to propose that the cross-endorsement provision be wiped from the books. A Democratic Party resolution considered briefly by party leaders denounced cross-endorsements saying: "The process has led to many cases where the people able to dispense such cross-endorsements obtain influence out of all proportion to the people they represent."[12] Similar sentiments have been expressed by the Republicans.[13]

Despite this current discontent, the major parties have learned to live with insurgent parties and factions (they first appeared on the scene at the turn of the century), which generally arose in reaction to disclosures of corrupt and autocratic major-party practices. Minor parties thus provided a vent for reformist zeal. But those minor parties that survived soon made their peace with the major parties. If major-party bosses had succeeded in suppressing dissident reformist parties, heightened public outrage might have cost the bosses control of their own party machines. The possibility of this occurring caused party leaders to at least tolerate the existence of these dissident elements.

These five factors outline a significant degree of electoral potency for minor parties; and the major parties decry the apparent extent of influence. Successful moves to change the system have been blocked, however, by a state legislature populated with representatives who have benefited from the system, and who are generally anxious to have their names appear on as many lines as possible, both because of the competitiveness of state party politics and because politicians perceive that an additional endorsement may make the critical difference in a close race. This cross-endorsement system has been viewed as both a positive and a negative force in state politics.[14] But whatever the normative assessment, this election law provision has served an indisputably important role in shaping the strategies and activities of the Right to Life Party.

NEW YORK'S MULTI-PARTY HISTORY

The unique multi-party nature of the state's electoral system traces its history back to an important change in ballot format in 1913—a change which also illustrates how electoral structures can shape electoral behavior.[15] The early twentieth century represented the high-water mark for Progressive influence, and consequent reformist pressures caused the state legislature to discontinue the party-column paper ballot voting system for statewide elections—a system that allowed voters to vote for an entire party slate if they checked a single circle at the top of the ballot. The new ballot system was the office-block paper ballot, which groups candidates by office. This new system left legislators with the problem of how to list cross-endorsed candidates (the cross-endorsement system was already a part of the political landscape). Under the old party-column system, cross-endorsed candidates appeared in each party column for which they received an endorsement. But the legislature decided that, in the 1914 statewide election, each name would appear only once (with names grouped by office), and voters would vote by marking the ballot with an "X" next to the party symbol appearing to the left of the candidate's name. Cross-endorsed candidates would have as many party symbols to the left of their names as they had party endorsements. On the 1914 ballot, party symbols were arrayed from left to right, with the major parties located farthest left. This placement had the unintended consequence, however, of attracting a large minor-party vote for cross-endorsed candidates, since voters tended to check the party symbol closest to the name, rather than that farthest to the left. Realizing their error, party leaders reversed the party symbol order, placing the major-party symbols to the immediate left of the candidate names, starting in 1916. As a consequence of this change, minor-party vote declined precipitously, and all but two minor parties disappeared. Yet minor-party fortunes revived with two important events in the 1930s: the American Labor Party's endorsement of Democrat Herbert H. Lehman for governor, and the increasingly widespread use of the voting machine (made mandatory by 1938). The significance of this latter change rests with the fact that the New York voting machine arrays candidates by party rows (see Figure 2.1), so that voters wanting to vote a straight party ticket need only pull the levers of that party's row. Unlike the office-block paper ballot, a cross-endorsed candidate's name appeared in the row of each party granting an endorsement. Thus, voting machines ironically

Figure 2.1
The New York State General Election Ballot, 1982

1 / 3 GOVERNOR & LIEUTENANT GOVERNOR (Vote Once)	4 COMPTROLLER (Vote for One)	5 ATTORNEY GENERAL (Vote for One)	6 UNITED STATES SENATOR (Vote for One)	7 / 8 JUSTICE OF THE SUPREME COURT 6th Judicial District (Vote for Any Two)		9 REPRESENTATIVE IN CONGRESS 28 (Vote for One)	10 STATE SENATOR 50 (Vote for One)	11 MEMBER OF ASSEMBLY 125 (Vote for One)
1A DEMOCRATIC Mario M. Cuomo / Alfred B. DelBello	4A DEMOCRATIC Raymond F Gallagher	5A DEMOCRATIC Robert Abrams	6A DEMOCRATIC Daniel P Moynihan	7A DEMOCRATIC Salvatore A Fauci	8A DEMOCRATIC William Tucker Dean	9A DEMOCRATIC Matt McHugh	10A DEMOCRATIC Richard J Shay	11A DEMOCRATIC John J Winkelman
1B REPUBLICAN Lew Lehrman / James L. Emery	4B REPUBLICAN Edward V Regan	5B REPUBLICAN Frances A Sclafani	6B REPUBLICAN Florence M Sullivan	7B REPUBLICAN D Bruce Crew	8B REPUBLICAN Albert E Tait, Jr.	9B REPUBLICAN David F Crowley	10B REPUBLICAN Lloyd S Riford, Jr.	11B REPUBLICAN Hugh S MacNeil
1C CONSERVATIVE Lew Lehrman / James L. Emery	4C CONSERVATIVE Edward V Regan	5C CONSERVATIVE Frances A Sclafani	6C CONSERVATIVE Florence M Sullivan	7C CONSERVATIVE Salvatore A Fauci	8C CONSERVATIVE Albert E Tait, Jr.	9C CONSERVATIVE David F Crowley	10C CONSERVATIVE Lloyd S Riford, Jr.	
1D RIGHT TO LIFE Robert J. Bohner / Paul F. Callahan	4D RIGHT TO LIFE John A Boyle	5D RIGHT TO LIFE Kevin P McGovern	6D RIGHT TO LIFE Florence M Sullivan			9D RIGHT TO LIFE Mark R Masterson		
1E LIBERAL Mario M. Cuomo / Alfred B. DelBello	4E LIBERAL William Finneran	5E LIBERAL Robert Abrams	6E LIBERAL Daniel P. Moynihan			9E LIBERAL Matt McHugh		
1F FREE LIBERTARIAN John H. Northrup / David Hoesly	4F FREE LIBERTARIAN William P McMillen	5F FREE LIBERTARIAN Dolores Grande	6F FREE LIBERTARIAN James J McKeown					
1G SOCIALIST WORKER Diane Wang / Peter A. Thierjung			6G SOCIALIST WORKER Steven Wattenmaker					
1H NEW ALLIANCE Nancy Ross / Lenora B. Fulani								
1I UNITY Jane Benedict / Angela M. Gilliam	3I INDEPENDENT Lew Lehrman / James L. Emery							11I CITIZENS Tim Joseph

helped encourage both party voting and the revival of minor-party lines attributable mostly to cross-endorsements.[16] As Howard Scarrow observes, various research and political experience demonstrate that allowing each party to have its own line is instrumental to the fortunes of those parties, both for the recognition it provides and for the way it facilitates calculating a party's contribution to a cross-endorsed candidate.[17]

One additional important change occurred in state regulations in 1947. Up until that time, nothing in New York law prevented one party's candidate from entering the primary race of another party, against the wishes of the latter party's leaders, and stealing away that nomination. This party "raiding" rarely occurred in New York (though it happened more frequently in states like California), but a celebrated case of a minor-party leader successfully "raiding" a congressional nomination from both the Republicans and the Democrats in 1942 eventually prompted the passage of the Wilson-Pakula Law. It said simply that a candidate only had the right to enter the primary of the party in which he or she was enrolled. A candidate could seek an additional party nod only with the consent of that party's governing committee. This 1947 law was initially viewed as a major blow to the minor parties.[18] In fact, it had the reverse effect by preventing the more likely prospect of major-party candidates attempting to raid the minor parties. In addition, it placed a major bargaining tool in the hands of party leaders (especially of the minor parties); that is, it allowed leaders the option of formally bestowing their party's endorsement, which could then serve as a basis for interparty bargaining. And the smaller, more homogeneous minor parties were and are in the best position to make such bargains, since control from the top is both more likely and more feasible than it is in the major parties.[19]

In sum, three artifacts of state law—cross-endorsement, ballot placement, and the no-raid provision—have all served to fortify the role of minor parties in New York. The state's electoral competitiveness has clearly provided fertile ground for the minor parties. Yet it is also abundantly clear that no such system would exist without appropriate state law, just as the absence of these kinds of provisions explains the absence of minor parties in other electorally competitive states.

Figure 2.2
New York State's Five Recognized Party Lines, 1982–1986

Enrollment

Name of Voter _____

Registration No. _____   Address _____

Date _____   City or Town _____

　　Legislative District _____ Ward _____   Election District _____

I hereby state that I am in general sympathy with the principles of the party which I have designated by my mark hereunder.

DEMOCRATIC   REPUBLICAN   CONSERVATIVE   LIBERAL   RIGHT TO LIFE

　　　○　　　　　○　　　　　○　　　　○　　　　○

INSTRUCTIONS

Make a cross X mark or a check ✓ mark with a pencil or pen in the circle under the emblem of the party with which you wish to enroll. Persons not wishing to enroll in a political party are to sign the form unmarked. Marks in more than one circle, will void the enrollment.

VOID

_____
Signature

THE "OTHER" PARTIES

New York has witnessed the emergence of no fewer than a dozen minor parties during the twentieth century.[20] Of this dozen, three maintain an automatic slot for all elections on the state ballot through 1986. These three, in order of formation, are the Liberal Party, the Conservative Party, and the Right to Life Party. (Figure 2.2 depicts a copy of the state's party enrollment form, giving the enrollment choices available to voters through 1986.)

The oldest of these, the Liberal Party, was an offshoot of the American Labor Party (ALP). The latter was formed by a group of socialists and trade unionists seeking a way to support President Roosevelt and other liberal candidates without working through the corrupt Democratic Party, then dominated by Tammany Hall.[21] The success of the Labor Party in bargaining with the major parties was such that it attracted more radical elements, including Communists, and in 1943 many of the original founders, including Alex Rose, broke away and formed the Liberal Party. Dominated by Rose until his death in 1976, the Liberal Party has generally sided with liberal Democratic candidates, though it did support a number of moderate Republicans in the 1960s.

The Conservative Party was also founded as a result of dissatisfaction with a major party. After his election as governor in 1958, Nelson Rockefeller dominated New York's Republican Party until 1974, when he resigned to become vice-president. But Rockefeller's brand of liberal Republicanism was distasteful to many traditional conservative Republicans, especially in the business and professional class, and a group of them combined in 1961 to offer a conservative alternative to Rockefeller Republicanism. They also hoped to pressure the Republicans to move to the right.[22] The Conservatives have generally identified with conservative Republicans, especially after Rockefeller's departure.

The Right to Life Party (RTLP) is the most recent entrant into the party fray. Even though the party is consciously narrow in its focus and recent in its origin, it would be a mistake to dismiss the RTLP case simply as a quirkish by-product of state law. To do so sidesteps the major issues raised by the existence of the party. First, given that the state party system encourages the perpetuation of minor parties once they have overcome the fairly substantial barriers to ballot access, how does the RTLP perform, and why did it succeed in obtaining a slot where other parties have not? Second, this party still represents a component, albeit an electoral one, of a larger political and social movement. Its adaptation to the vagaries of New York election law ought not to disqualify it from analysis. Third, as the description of the RTLP's evolution will reveal, the efforts of the group's leadership to enter electoral politics was not prompted solely by the cross-endorsement provision in New York law, since their initial efforts, at both the state and federal level, involved attempts to work through the major parties. For these reasons, the RTLP provides an excellent opportunity to examine the workings of a nascent political party. Moreover, New York's minor parties can be best understood as a part of America's third-party tradition.

A recent landmark study of third parties has done much to fill the theoretical gap in our understanding of minor parties.[23]

This major work examines important national third-party movements of the past, especially as evidenced in third-party presidential challenges, and explicates a theory of third-party voting. Though this study provides considerable insight into third-partyism, its focus on presidentially centered third-party efforts yields a narrow perspective on minor-party development. Moreover, it analytically separates major parties from minor parties; I argue that, both empirically and normatively, it is desirable to approach minor parties in the same way one approaches the development of major parties (while recognizing obvious differences). More specifically, the theory of third-party voting explicated by Rosenstone, Behr, and Lazarus identifies three key factors that determine the existence and level of third-party support: the presence of major-party deterioration, attractive minor-party candidates who can rally support for a small party, and a rise in voters lacking major-party loyalties.[24] Yet not one of these three conditions holds for the case of the RTLP. Moreover, our interest extends beyond third-party voting behavior to that of party leaders, institutional factors, and social conditions. Given this fact, and the normative arguments to be made in a subsequent chapter about minor parties, an alternate theoretical approach becomes highly desirable.

A DYNAMIC MODEL OF THIRD PARTIES

The RTLP is by no means unique as a case of popular discontent expressed through a third-party movement. It is in fact part of a long tradition of electoral activity outside of the two major parties. In the interest of establishing the commonalities between this and other third-party movements, a dynamic model of third parties will be applied to the RTLP case. The model synthesizes the work of much third-party analysis.[25] It consists of three temporal stages. These stages, however, are predicated upon a series of five assumptions.

First, individuals must believe that a discontented group exists among the electorate, based on some failure of the existing system to cope with the relevant discontent. Second, third parties pose a viable electoral alternative (as opposed to lobbying, etc.).

These parties accumulate votes to either win elections or affect major party behavior. But in either instance, third-party germination is closely dependent on the fertility of rules and structures that regulate parties, candidates and elections. Third, the degree of electoral success is a major benchmark for assessing the developmental stage of a party. Fourth, third parties should be studied as though they were major parties. Fifth, the development of third parties is a "value-added" process. "Every stage . . . is a necessary condition for the appropriate and effective addition of value in the next stage."[26] Thus, events follow a temporal sequence.

Stage I of the model incorporates the period of social unrest. During this period, the normal structures of society are not responsive to a particular need or point of view, and groups seek to achieve their ends by the accumulation of votes. Some segment of the population is discontented, and thus a variety of organizational forms associated with the movement spring up, such as associations, interest groups, and major-party insurgencies. The third party is but one of these forms. Specifically, one might also look for civil disorder, movements within major-party coalitions and attempts to use state parties to achieve national ends.

During Stage II, the third-party organization tries to translate discontent into support at the polls. This translation is related to three factors. First, the actions of the two major parties and their candidates will determine what proportion of the social movement cannot find a home within one of the major parties.

The second factor related to the proportion of the social movement transferred to the polls is the ability and quality of the third party's organization, candidate, and campaign. The focus here is on the leadership, the activist cadres, and the voters, in terms of how and in what ways they support the party. The background of the leaders (have they held office before?) affects whether the party is outer-directed toward the electorate, or inner-directed toward the needs and issues of the activists. If the leaders are outer-directed, they will be interested in maximizing the vote. They will seek a tight organizational structure to control the zealots who would alienate new, potential voters. If leaders are inner-directed, their primary interest will be in

maintaining party integrity (homogeneity or purity). Party activists may be attracted and motivated by a variety of incentives,
including issue/purposive, material, solidarity (feelings of civic
obligation to the community), and candidate. The party needs
activists motivated by purposive incentives to overcome major
obstacles, but if they are dominant, the party will turn inward
and become increasingly dogmatic, thus encouraging an inner-
directed party. If the activists are motivated by material or can-
didate-loyalty incentives, the party will be more outer-directed.
Voters will be attracted to the third party by either candidates
or issues. If the attraction is the former, a candidate may have
the opportunity to counter the party's extremist image and attract more votes (often beyond the bounds of the social
movement).

The third factor influencing the translation of discontent is the
receptivity and response of institutions and structures. If institutional barriers, frustrations, and hurdles are too great, the
movement will more readily seek other avenues of expression.
As sociologist Michael Useem has observed, "any theory of protest must take as a major analytic issue the relationship between
dissent and the state."[27]

Stage III incorporates the reaction to the party's electoral performance—specifically, its degree of electoral success, and the
reaction of the third party and the major parties to that success.
There are four possible electoral paths for a third party. The first
is that the third party receives an every-increasing percentage
of the vote, such that it supplants (replaces) one of the major
parties. Second, the third party might receive enough votes to
convince observers that, if its vote continues to increase at the
same rate, it will threaten the balance between the major parties.
In this instance, one or more of the major parties seeks to attract
votes from the minor party by adopting its issues and/or candidates. In the case of the third alternative, the third party at-
tracts an increasing, though not dramatic, percent of the vote,
but the vote then stabilizes and begins to decline as a percent
of the total vote. After some initial interest, the major parties
ignore the new party. Finally, a third party may attract a small
vote from the beginning, which then stabilizes and/or gets

smaller. When this occurs, the major parties are likely to ignore the third party.

APPLICATION

Stage I

With the enactment of a liberalized abortion law in New York in 1970, and the Supreme Court rulings in *Roe v. Wade* and *Doe v. Bolton* (1973) the prevailing public policy has been one of providing women the opportunity to obtain abortions at their own discretion, especially in the early months of pregnancy. Inroads have been made against this prevailing policy at all levels of government, but the basic policy thrust remains that articulated in *Roe*.[28] Thus, the normal structures of society have been mostly unresponsive to the perspectives of abortion opponents, insofar as women can still obtain elective abortions if they have the money.

One might consider the Hyde Amendment (prohibiting the use of federal Medicaid funds for abortions), the enactment of abortion-restricting legislation in at least a dozen states, and the much-touted defeat of some pro-choice legislators (such as Senators Dick Clark of Iowa and Frank Church of Idaho) as evidences that the system is responding to right-to-life pressures. Yet it is the nature of this single-issue movement that compromises and halfway measures do not suffice. As one party leader commented, "There would be no reason for us to exist if we made concessions on the very issue that's so important to us." According to Paul Brown, head of the Life Amendment Political Action Committee, "Our [candidate] ratings are 100 percent or zero. . . . There's no middle ground."[29] In the eyes of right-to-life activists, then, the system has not been or will be considered "responsive" until the prevailing doctrine reverts back to the prohibition of abortion.[30] In the context of this perceived governmental unresponsiveness, the RTLP has evolved as a structure to accumulate votes—though not with the intent of winning elections, as the discussion of party strategy will make clear.

The perceived lack of system responsiveness leads naturally

to the question of discontent itself. Who and how many are discontented in the population, and how strongly do they feel? This question can be addressed in two ways: first, by citing opinion polls, and second, by assessing the depth and intensity of feelings about the issue among the public activists.

Public opinion concerning abortion as a public issue is notoriously difficult to gauge, both because an individual's personal moral convictions do not necessarily equate directly into evident preferences for governmental actions, and because question wording affects poll results. Yet, it has been studied exhaustively.[31] Opinion questions usually center on the circumstances under which respondents would or would not permit abortions. These circumstances range from "hard" (allowing abortion in instances of rape, incest, life of the mother) to "soft" (mother's mental health, mother unmarried, or pregnancy otherwise unwanted) instances. In brief summary, findings vary, but in general roughly 10 to 20 percent of the population oppose abortions under any circumstances, while an equivalent or slightly larger proportion favor allowing abortions under all circumstances.[32] Comparison of responses to NORC opinion questions over the space of 15 years (1965–1980) indicates that nationwide approval of abortion has increased during this period in all categories.[33] Despite variations in question wording and interpretation, most Americans agree that abortions should be allowed under at least some circumstances (including "soft" circumstances) and that women should be allowed to decide for themselves whether they will obtain an abortion. A 1984 *New York Times*/CBS Poll reported on public reaction to proposed attempts to amend the Constitution to curtail abortion practices. Sixty-three percent opposed an amendment that would make all abortions illegal (28 percent in favor); 48 percent opposed an amendment allowing abortions only to save the life of the mother (43 percent in favor). Yet, as Table 2.1 shows, the public is widely tolerant of abortion in many circumstances, such as when the possibility of serious birth defects exists, and when the health of the mother is jeopardized. Opinions split more evenly for circumstances hinging more directly on the discretion of the woman.

The determinants of abortion attitudes have been linked to demographic, psychological, political and moral factors.[34] Our

Table 2.1
Percent Agreeing That Abortion Should Be Legal, 1972–1984

	1972	1974	1976	1978	1980	1982	1984
if there is a strong chance there is a serious defect in the baby	79%	85%	84%	82%	83%	85%	80%
if a woman is married, and doesn't want any more children	40	47	46	40	47	48	43
if the woman's own health is endangered by the pregnancy	87	92	91	91	90	92	90
if the family has very low income and cannot afford any more children	49	55	53	47	52	52	46
if a woman became pregnant as a result of a rape	79	87	84	83	83	87	80
if a woman is not married and doesn't want to marry the man	44	50	50	41	48	49	44

Source: National Opinion Research Center. See John Herbers, "Abortion Issue Threatens to Become Profoundly Divisive," New York Times, October 14, 1984.

concern, however, is not with mass attitudes toward abortion, but rather with the political and policy consequences of those attitudes.

More germane is the question of issue intensity. As previously mentioned, a Peter Hart poll revealed that a quarter of those surveyed would vote against an incumbent solely on the basis of his/her stand on abortion. Other research concludes that "even though the opponents [of abortion] are numerically few . . . they are much more willing to vote on the basis of a single issue than are the more numerous proponents. This differential intensity is more marked for the abortion issue where one-third of the 'pro-lifers' were willing to base their vote on that issue alone."[35] President Reagan's campaign pollster, Richard Wirthlin, estimated that only one voter in ten votes based on the abortion issue, but that most of these people tend to oppose abortion.[36]

Societal discontent with prevailing abortion policy is not numerically widespread, but it is intense among many who oppose the practice. Moreover, as many have noted, there is no "middle ground" for those falling into this category. Individuals who identify strongly with the right-to-life cause maintain an unwavering moral commitment founded in opposition to an act understood by them to be murder.[37]

A final element of the stage of social unrest is evidenced in the existence of multiple forms of political expression. The RTLP is but one of a multitude of groups seeking to curtail the practice of abortion. At least three types of conventional political organizations have sprung up since the 1970s. The oldest type of organization is the educational group. Right-to-Life Committees exist at all levels, with the stated purpose of "educating" society (but including decision makers) about the evils of abortion. These groups usually operate on a nonprofit, tax-exempt basis, relying principally on publications, from newsletters and periodicals to color pamphlets graphically depicting aborted fetuses.

A second type of group incorporates lobby and political action committee (PAC) organizations. These groups contribute money to pro-life candidates and incumbents, and lobby in Washington and state capitals for favorable legislation and for a constitutional amendment banning abortions. The third organizational pattern incorporates those attempting to actually enter decision-making circles—principally through party activity, by running candidates and working in campaigns (both major- and minor-party).

A final, more exotic variety of political expression also denotes social unrest. It is evidenced in the extra-legal activities of anti-abortion individuals and fringe groups, including arson and bombing of abortion clinics, kidnapping, assault, death threats and harassment. The FBI reported at least 23 bombing and arson incidents against abortion facilities in 1984, compared to two in 1983 and three in 1982.[38] Such incidents obviously involved very small numbers of people either acting alone or with some kind of nominal group affiliation (notably, the "Army of God"). Yet the relative rarity of political violence in America draws even greater attention to such fringe incidents, precisely because of the intensity of feeling generating such acts. Also, these extreme actions have served to rivet national attention. As one nonviolent right-to-life activist observed, the bombings "negative though they are, have actually helped the anti-abortion cause by bringing attention to the issue. All of a sudden it's on the cover of *Newsweek*. It's on '20–20.' "[39]

The right-to-life movement, though hampered by splits and often sharp disputes, nevertheless shares a commonality of purpose that has attracted as many as 10 million adherents to its cause.[40] One need not provide a laundry list of right-to-life organizations to be convinced that the movement is organizationally active and diverse. In political terms, the social unrest is sufficiently widespread and intense to have kept the issue in the political foreground since the early 1970s. The probable absence of a numerical majority of committed right-to-lifers among people in the country in no way negates their political importance. The same can be said in particular of those right-to-lifers who have engaged in party activity.

Stage II

The evolution of the Right to Life Party can be viewed as distinct reaction to the lack of responsiveness of the major parties, at both the national and state levels, to the sentiments of abortion opponents. The history of the New York RTLP exemplifies this major party disinterest and the partisan response it provoked. *A third party is born.* In this age of Madison Avenue media campaign consultants, multi-million dollar political action committees, and high-powered political organizing and recruiting drives, one cannot help but be impressed at the inauspicious grassroots origins of the RTLP. The party's antecedents can be traced to a book-discussion group composed of Merrick, Long Island housewives. In 1969, much attention was being paid to the attempt in the state legislature to enact a liberalized abortion law. (In all, 18 states liberalized their abortion laws during the decade of the 1960s.) The women in the discussion group discovered a shared antipathy to abortion, and decided that they would lobby against the bill in Albany. Despite the efforts of this group and other, better-organized abortion opponents, New York enacted its liberalized abortion law in 1970.[41] Far from discouraging abortion opponents, the new law, and similar actions in other states, prompted the women to enter the political realm in a large way. In the words of Ellen McCormack, a party founder and its presidential candidate in 1976 and 1980, "decisions were being made by the politicians that had a tremendous control over our lives . . . we realized that the leaders in this country were giving a direction to society that we didn't benefit by. We felt that it [liberalized abortion legislation] was an intrusion in our lives and the lives of young children, and they were getting control over our lives that frightened us."

Sweeping concerns of this nature often spring from a background of prior political commitment consistent with what is known about political activists.[42] Yet the backgrounds of many of the RTLP leaders are indisputably apolitical (aside from engaging in voting). The case of Mrs. McCormack is illustrative. Brought up in New York City, McCormack (high school educated at a Catholic parochial school, no college) has lived in suburban New York, married to a retired New York City deputy policy inspector. She is the mother of four. Though involved in school and neighborhood activities, she had no prior experience in politics until this time. The concerns of people like McCormack

accelerated when the Supreme Court rendered its decision in
Roe.[43]

This right-to-life group's initial foray into politics involved
attempts to operate both as an independent group and through
the major parties. Party leaders date the formation of their party
to 1970, when they attempted to run two candidates for office.
An unsuccessful attempt was made to run Jane Gilroy for governor; running into New York's stiff ballot access regulations,
Gilroy's nominating petitions were disqualified. They did succeed, however, in entering Vincent Carey as a congressional
candidate in New York's Fifth Congressional District, against
incumbent Democrat Allard Lowenstein, who was himself
ousted by Republican Norman Lent. Lent's margin of victory
was only about 10,000 votes, and, as Ellen McCormack tells it,
Lent began supporting the right-to-life position at this time at
least partly because Carey received 5,000 votes. As McCormack
said, "even though we lost the election, we felt we had been
successful."[44]

In 1974, this group worked actively for the New York Conservative Party's candidate for U.S. Senate, Barbara Keating. In
its advertisements, Keating's campaign focused primarily on the
single issue of abortion. Keating's showing of 16 percent in the
fall election prompted the right-to-life people to claim that "abortion is a major issue with the voters."[45] It also helped persuade
them that entrance into electoral politics was more fruitful than
traditional lobbying and educational efforts.

In 1976, McCormack ran an avowedly single-issue campaign
(though she announced positions on other issues later) as a
Democrat in that party's presidential primaries. She received a
total of 238,000 votes in 18 primary states, acquiring 22 convention delegate votes. In the process, she qualified for federal
matching funds by raising the minimum of $5,000 in each of 20
states, as prescribed by the Federal Election Commission. In all,
her campaign raised $285,000, which was matched by $247,000
in federal funds. More than half of this was spent on TV
advertisements.[46]

Using vote totals and money raised as indicators, the Mc-
Cormack campaign was something less than a success.[47] But this

perspective belies what emerged as the primary electoral tactic of the soon-to-be-formed RTLP. Even during the Democratic primaries, right-to-life strategists sought to crystallize "a fiery minority and a new cadre of leaders who will vote their anti-abortion feelings single-mindedly, regardless of other issues or old party attachments."[48] Small percentages do not win elections, but they can tip the political balance scales among those major candidates who do possess winning capabilities. More importantly, major party candidates often perceive the small vote percentages of minor candidates as important, if not crucial, to the outcome of a race. This yields a minor-party strategy based on bargaining and "blackmail" with respect to the major parties, rather than the threat of winning elections outright. This becomes an especially salient strategy in New York politics because of the cross-endorsement rule. Despite what some considered a promising showing by a political unknown, this right-to-life group opted out of major-party channels, and in 1978 succeeded in placing Mary Jane Tobin, a party founder, on the ballot as a gubernatorial candidate (McCormack ran for lieutenant governor). The leaders had decided that working within the major parties was fruitless, since neither was perceived as responsive to the right-to-life perspective.

The organizers were careful this time to obtain far more signatures than necessary. The requirement for ballot access for statewide office stipulates that a candidate not running in a recognized party must obtain at least 20,000 petition signatures from independent voters, with at least 100 from each of one-half of the state's congressional districts. This time, the party succeeded in soliciting more than twice as many signatures (54,000) for Tobin's gubernatorial candidacy. In the general election, she received 130,193 votes statewide, or 2.6 percent of all votes cast—more than the Liberal Party received for its gubernatorial candidate, Hugh Carey. This gave the RTLP the fourth spot on the ballot, ahead of the Liberals, in all elections until 1982, since party position on the ballot is determined by gubernatorial vote.

Tobin's showing, founded on a campaign budget of about $70,000, was considered a substantial success. The establishment of this ballot line has prompted a proliferation of RTLP candidacies and endorsements at the state and local level. In 1979, the party claimed that it had endorsed over 600 candidates for office, though many of them were cross-endorsements.

In 1980, the party split on its presidential endorsement, but finally opted for McCormack (the National Right-to-Life Committee split with the party and endorsed Reagan). Right-to-lifers from upstate preferred Reagan as the party nominee, but the majority of party leaders turned away from Reagan for several reasons. First, Reagan's staff made no attempt to seek the RTLP endorsement until literally the eleventh hour. According to party officials interviewed, the nomination could have been his for the asking earlier on. Second, many were dismayed by his selection of George Bush as a running mate. Reagan's right-to-life stand was not unblemished (in the 1960s he had signed a bill liberalizing abortion laws in California), but Bush was perceived as being clearly pro-choice. Also, McCormack expressed consternation at Reagan's political support of pro-choice Republicans like Charles Percy of Illinois and Jacob Javits in New York.[49] Third, Reagan had confused the proposed Human Life Amendment with the Hyde Amendment in his discussions with party officials, and this also turned away support. Since the urge to put up someone exceeded sentiments to leave the line blank, McCormack was nominated, despite fears that she would pull votes away from Reagan.[50] McCormack appeared on the ballot in three states (NY, NJ, and KY), and received 32,327 votes (24,159 in NY). Party successes at the state and local level were more marked.

Statewide contests. The RTLP's first major statewide test after gaining the number four ballot spot occurred in 1980. With all 220 members of the state legislature up for reelection, as well as 39 congressional seats and a U.S. Senate race, party leaders were anxious to make a good showing. To this end, RTLP leaders expressed a clear preference for endorsing major-party candidates for office over running candidates possessing only the RTLP endorsement. In the race for the Senate, Republican Alphonse D'Amato received 152,470 votes on the RTLP line, or 2.4 percent of all votes cast. This total exceeded his margin of victory over his Democratic opponent, thereby fostering the RTLP claim that it had elected D'Amato. (The Conservative Party made the same claim, though, as it had endorsed D'Amato first, and garnered more votes for him than the RTLP.)

In 1982, party fortunes turned downward in the key statewide race. The RTLP again fielded its own candidate, a downstate lawyer named Robert Bohner. He received 52,356 votes (0.96 percent of the vote cast), just barely enough to keep the RTLP on the ballot through 1986. In the Senate race that year, the party endorsed the Republican nominee, Florence Sullivan. Though soundly defeated by Democrat incumbent Daniel P. Moynihan, she still received 105,367 votes on the RTLP line (1.9 percent of votes cast), about double Bohner's total. As a result of Bohner's poor showing, the party's ballot position slipped from fourth to fifth.

In 1984, the RTLP decided at its convention not to endorse anyone for president. McCormack said that "Reagan is for therapeutic abortion . . . to protect the physical and mental health of the mother. . . . We don't condone abortion under any circumstances."[51] The consistent anti-Reagan position of the party has been a matter of concern to many party activists, who feel that this stand runs contrary to the wishes of many party members, as well as most other right-to-lifers. Concern about the perceived extremism of the RTLP prompted some party leaders to form the Committee to Revitalize the Right to Life Party. The purpose of this intra-party group was to bring the party closer to the "center," and to promote the party's endorsement of Ronald Reagan for president at the September RTLP convention in Albany. The decision not to endorse Reagan followed an intense intra-party struggle between the centrists and the ruling Long Island group, headed by Tobin and McCormack. The decision to endorse no candidate (unlike 1980) was explained by one party activist as a case where any endorsement other than Reagan "would have been a disaster." The weighted voting system within the party allows the Long Island party leaders to maintain control over the party structure and agenda, and this has been a source of frustration to party activists from New York City and upstate who feel that the party has become, in the words of one activist, "more and more tight and exclusionary." One activist in particular described several proposals made at the party convention to improve intra-party communication and to improve the party's image. All were rejected by the party leaders, according to the activist, because they said they would not be able to maintain adequate control. The activist interviewed questioned the propriety and necessity of this degree of control. As the activist ruefully observed, "any 'reaching out' is considered a betrayal of the party." Another observed that the leaders' actions "are going to lead to the end of the pro-life party." One country chairman said, after announcing his forthcoming resignation, "I'm convinced that—although I'm still pro-life—the Right to Life Party is not in the best interest of the pro-life cause."

State legislative contests. The electoral fortunes of the RTLP are gauged far more clearly by the multiplicity of contests for the state legislature and Congress. The legislature is important both because it bears the collective responsibility for passage of New York's liberal abortion law in 1970 (and has thus been the main focus of state right-to-life pressures), and because it provides 632 separate races (for senate and assembly across three election years) in which the RTLP has attempted to exert influence. The 107 House of Representatives elections provide additional opportunities for the party—and for analysis.

Despite the stated RTLP preference for endorsing major-party candidates, Table 2.2 makes clear that most ballot slots were filled with candidates whose sole endorsement was the RTLP. Also, endorsements of Republicans far exceeded those of other party candidates. Comparison across the years reveals a uniform downward trend in number of solely RTLP candidates, and in the number of cross-endorsements (though the latter decline is more precipitous than the former). It also lends indirect support for a proposition heard informally from the RTLP critics— namely, that despite the desire of major-party candidates to obtain as many lines as possible, many not only resist RTLP pressures but in fact consider an endorsement from this more extreme party a stigma rather than a plus.

Even though the RTLP is endorsing fewer candidates, it could be the case that its vote percentages are holding steady. Yet Table 2.3 reveals this not to be so. A comparison of mean vote totals reveals the relatively greater drawing power of a major-party candidate also listed on a minor-party line. In 1980, the RTLP seemed to draw about one percent more of the vote when

Table 2.2
New York State Races Since the Advent of the Right to Life Party: 1980–1984

	U.S. House of Reps.			State Senate			State Assembly		
	1980	1982	1984	1980	1982	1984	1980	1982	1984
number of seats up	39	34	34	60	61	61	150	150	150
total number of candidates endorsed by RTLP	35	22	19	49	39	27	116	85	72
number of candidates listed solely on RTLP line	16	14	9	24	24	22	47	42	41
number of candidates endorsed by Reps. and RTLP[a]	14	6	10	14	11	5	55	29	23
number of candidates endorsed by Dems. and RTLP	0	0	0	5	1	0	2	8	4
number of candidates endorsed by Cons. and RTLP	4	2	0	4	2	0	4	7	4
number of candidates endorsed by Reps., Dems., and RTLP	0	0	0	5	0	0	2	0	0

[a]Includes candidates endorsed by Conservatives as well.
Data drawn from New York State Board of Elections.

Table 2.3
Aggregate Right to Life Party Vote: 1980–1984

	U.S. House of Reps.			State Senate			State Assembly		
	1980	1982	1984	1980	1982	1984	1980	1982	1984
1. Mean RTLP vote for candidates with major party endorsement	3.4%	2.3%	1.9%	3.5%	3.0%	2.7%	3.6%	2.8%	2.3%
A. downstate mean	a	a	a	3.9	3.3	2.7	3.7	3.1	2.4
					(districts 1–38)		(districts 1–98)	(districts 1–97)	
B. upstate mean	a	a	a	3.2	2.3	0	3.3	2.3	2.1
					(districts 39–60 c)		(districts 99–150)	(districts 98–150)	
2. Mean RTLP vote for candidates holding only RTLP Line b	2.3	1.9	1.8	2.6	2.2	2.3	2.3	2.4	2.3
A. downstate mean	a	a	a	2.6	2.3	2.1	2.3	2.6	2.2
B. upstate mean	a	a	a	2.5	1.9	2.7	2.3	1.5	2.9

a Upstate-downstate breakdowns are omitted because of the smaller number of cases.
b Also includes candidates endorsed by conservative Party.
c The State Senate has had 61 districts since 1982.
Data drawn from New York State Board of Elections

it endorsed a major-party candidate than when it ran one of its own. Yet by 1984, this gap had consistently narrowed, if not disappeared for congressional, state senate and state assembly races. The party has thus apparently lost voters who supported the RTLP only when it ran a major-party candidate.

Second, the RTLP has suffered a persistent, consistent vote drain from 1980 to 1984 in all categories. This fact likely damages the party's claim that it provides the crucial vote in many close races. In 1980, only two contests (both for state assembly) were determined by less than the RTLP vote total (aside from D'Amato's senate race). In 1982, there were three such races (one each for Congress, state senate, and assembly). In 1984, there were none. If we compare upstate with downstate percentages, we can see that RTLP cross-endorsed candidates ran somewhat better downstate than upstate, whereas candidates solely on the RTLP line evidenced no consistent pattern. (The party ran about the same proportion of candidates upstate as downstate.) The consequences of these trends will be discussed more fully in the "Stage III" evaluation.

The RTLP and the political environment. The preceding detailed chronology serves as a basis for assessing the dynamics of this third-party movement in relation to the major parties. First, the initial electoral thrusts of this right-to-life group included attempts to work through existing parties. Second, these attempts proved fruitless in terms of either acquiring enough votes to sway party leaders or at least attracting sufficient notice and support within the parties. Indeed, RTLP activists interviewed complained again and again that though many politicians expressed sympathy for the right-to-life cause, few were willing to adopt aggressive public stands. The major parties themselves, especially at the state level, were and are considered to be even less responsive. The frustrations of party activists were typified by the comments of one RTLP leader who complained that he had been told by several local public officials and political opponents that his and the party's activities would be simply ignored by them.

Leading major party figures at both the state and national level at first avoided raising the abortion issue in the public forum, or at the very least have not sought to draw out their opponents on the issue. Republican and Democratic national party platforms made no reference to abortion until 1976, when the Republican platform adopted some mildly anti-abortion language and the Democrats some mildly pro-choice language. In 1980 and 1984, both party platforms included stands on abortion, with Republicans taking a stronger pro-life stand, and Democrats a strong pro-choice position.[52]

At the state level, far less movement on abortion has been evidenced. State Democratic Party leaders have generally supported New York's liberalized laws (including Medicaid funding), as have many Republican leaders. The two major-party gubernatorial candidates in 1978 were both perceived as insensitive to right-to-life concerns, as had been the case in prior years.[53] In 1982, Democrat Mario Cuomo was also strongly pro-choice (Catholic-Italian heritage notwithstanding). The Republican candidate, Lewis Lehrman, identified himself as right-to-life but opposed legislation to outlaw abortion. He was nevertheless endorsed by the state's Right-to-Life Committee for his support of a cutoff in Medicaid funding for abortion. Lehrman also sent out a mass mailing during the campaign directed at currying favor with right-to-life voters. These intra-movement disputes lent some credence to RTLP charges that its gubernatorial candidate's vote total was artificially deflated.[54] Other state races reinforce this impression, as RTLP candidates for comptroller and attorney general received 76,000 and 101,000 votes respectively (neither was cross-endorsed).

The main point is that the major parties have moved slowly, even grudgingly, to cleave along the abortion issue. In particular, many in the right-to-life movement continue to voice dissatisfaction with candidates like Lehrman and Ronald Reagan. Even enthusiastic Reagan supporters in the RTLP view Reagan with suspicion and cynicism, calculating that his sympathies are founded in political expediency more than ideological fervor.

The political course of action pursued by the RTLP has been shaped not only by the conditions, positions, and perspectives of the existing party structure, but also by the party's internal structure and motivation. It is to the question of organization and leadership, then, that we now turn.

The party and politics. The leadership of the RTLP shares one

primary characteristic—that of prior noninvolvement, if not disinterest in politics. The typical party activist had, prior to joining
the party, limited his/her political activities to voting. At some
point, they had become interested in the abortion issue and in
many cases had joined one or more of the numerous right-to-
life committees before entering party politics. As one party official commented, "I never was really politically motivated or
involved . . . but I have become deeply, deeply involved [in party
politics] because of the right-to-life movement." Similarly, the
stated commitment of these activists is limited to a resolution of
the abortion issue; that is, ending abortions. "As soon as we get
a human life amendment, I'm getting right back out of politics."
Leader sentiments are indeed fixed solely and singularly around
the single issue of abortion.[55] This single-issue fixation is reflected in the party's rules, which state three purposes: enactment of a constitutional amendment overturning *Roe*; advocacy
of legislation to regulate and restrict abortion, including the elim-
ination of public expenditures for abortions; and opposition to
efforts to promote euthanasia as it is defined in the party rules.

In addition to sharing non-activist backgrounds, the party
leaders interviewed (not a representative sample) also exhibited
certain other commonalities.[56] All but one leader interviewed
were Catholic (the exception was Mormon), and nearly all were
formerly registered as Democrats before joining the party. Two
had been registered independents, and one was a former
Republican.

The personal backgrounds of party leaders lead almost inev-
itably, according to the model, to a party which is inner-directed
toward the needs, issues and concerns of its activists, rather
than outer-directed toward the larger electorate. In other set-
tings, this overriding drive toward issue purity and party integrity would limit the party both numerically and strategically. In
New York, party size is hampered, but the party is able to maintain a viable strategic position by offering its endorsement as a
bargaining chip with other parties and candidates. Nevertheless,
the party's rigid adherence to the right-to-life position on abortion has prompted some consequences inimical to the movement's political standing. In the state capital, the RTLP has
earned a reputation for inflexibility that has resulted in the al-

ienation of right-to-life supporters.[57] For example, a Democratic state assemblyman from Queens, Vincent Nicolosi (an acknowledged right-to-life supporter and assembly leader on the issue), was confronted by party officials who threatened to run their own candidate against him because he refused to condemn Assembly Speaker Stanley Fink (pro-choice) for blocking more restrictive abortion legislation. Such condemnation by a party member would constitute a violation of legislative norms, since it would only serve to alienate himself from the leadership. According to Assemblyman Nicolosi, "I think the Right to Life Party loses credibility when they take 100 percent agreement as the only yardstick by which they measure you."[58] A freshman conservative Republican assemblywoman, Joan Hague, was similarly put off by RTLP tactics. She claimed that she was open to persuasion on the issue but was incensed by their tactics. "They weren't even ladies. They brought in pictures of fetuses in garbage bags—to think they could gain my support by showing me pictures like that . . . they wouldn't listen to reason. They just screamed at me."[59] Some have argued that the RTLP endorsement has actually become a liability for candidates, and that even right-to-life sympathizers have declined the endorsement. In 1982 and 1984, for example, staunch right-to-life incumbent Republican State Senator James H. Donovan declined the party's nod.[60] In 1986, Republican gubernatorial nominee (and clear underdog) Andrew O'Rourke declined the RTLP endorsement, forcing the party to nominate Nassau County District Attorney Dennis Dillon.

The RTLP's dogmatism has provoked rifts not only with state politicians, but with other elements of the right-to-life movement as well. As mentioned, the RTLP split with the National Right-to-Life Committee by endorsing Ellen McCormack for president, instead of Reagan.[61] At the state level, differing goals and strategies have put the Right-to-Life Committee and Party at odds. During the 1980 state assembly session, the Right-to-Life Committee made a deal with pro-choice legislators to allow a bill limiting the availability of abortions for minors to reach the assembly floor, in exchange for a promise by the Right-to-Life Committee that it would not push for a vote on a national constitutional convention before next year's elections. Pro-life legislators who accepted the compromise were criticized by McCormack and were threatened with the loss of the party's endorsement.[62]

A rift exists between the party and New York's Right-to-Life PAC as well. The latter has declined to support the activities of the RTLP. It has refused to endorse or financially support any RTLP candidate not endorsed by the major parties. This split arose at least in part from the Right-to-Life PAC's opposition to the party's call for a constitutional convention ("con-con") as an alternate method of amending the Constitution. RTLP leaders interviewed had few kind words for the PAC. Thus, the RTLP and other such groups continue to be split over exactly how the goal of abortion abolition is to be reached.[63] One additional source of friction anticipated by many was between the RTLP and the Conservative Party, as both would ostensibly draw on similar constituencies. Yet the two parties have avoided divisive confrontations (the Conservative Party itself maintains no consistent stand on abortion, and was rejected early on as a home for the movement), apparently to the benefit of both. The Conservatives have maintained their number three ranking on the ballot, and the cross-endorsement rule eliminates the necessity for candidates to choose one endorsement over the other. Conflict avoidance is probably enhanced by the fact that the Conservative Party tends to draw from a different (especially more affluent upper-status suburban) constituency than the RTLP.[64]

The description of an ideologically rigid, inner-directed party yields a picture of activists and leaders motivated exclusively by ideological/purposive incentives. According to the model of party development, the prevalence of these incentives aids the party in its early development (as indeed it has), but constrains its growth beyond the limits set by the party's ideologues. On the basis of this assessment, we would expect the party to turn increasingly inward and dogmatic, and this indeed has been its course to the present, despite its reputed successes. In the absence of candidate-centered campaigns, voter appeal will continue to be centered along (and constrained by) fairly rigid ideological lines. But again, the nature of New York's electoral law system allows the RTLP to seek and obtain certain electoral benefits and rewards that may serve to perpetuate the party in its present form beyond what might otherwise be its normal lifespan.

Stage III

This final stage of the developmental cycle incorporates an assessment of the electoral success of the minor party, and the reactions of the major parties.

At the national level, the signs of right-to-life movement pressure are abundant. Beginning with the successful passage of the Hyde Amendment in 1976[65] and the Supreme Court's favorable ruling on the act in 1980 (*Harris v. McRae*), the embrace of the right-to-life issue by Reagan, the appointment of sympathetic administrators in the Reagan administration, and the serious consideration of a Human Life Amendment and Act in Congress, the direction of federal policy has clearly moved away from *Roe* principles. The existence and persistence of right-to-life pressure were acknowledged even before the Reagan administration by Carter's HEW Secretary, Joseph Califano, who observed that the abortion issue endlessly plagued both the president and HEW during Carter's term—and indeed was responsible for continually holding up appropriations bills in Congress.[66]

At the state level, no such movement has taken place, despite annual political struggles over abortion. RTLP leaders attribute this fact largely to the pro-choice sentiments of state party leaders, despite what they view as a rising chorus of opposition among others in the major parties. In the electoral arena, however, the party has succeeded in fielding and/or endorsing large numbers of candidates and acquiring a small, if slowly declining, percent of the vote. As previously noted, RTLP aggregate vote percents for state legislative contests have slowly eroded since the high point of 1980, as have the number of endorsed candidates. Despite this apparently pessimistic assessment of RTLP strength, the empirical strength of the party is, in many respects, less important than its reputational strength. An electoral strategy centering on political perceptions was voiced by a RTLP leader: "If you scare the hell out of one pro-abortion congressman or senator, you are going to convert ten others. They might be pro-abortion, but they don't feel that strongly about it." This was precisely the situation described by Margolis and Neary in their study of the Pennsylvania State Legislature and its members' responses to the abortion issue; that is, abortion was an issue of low salience to most legislators, and they opted to vote pro-life rather than risk the wrath, real or imagined, of the right-to-lifers.[67]

Naturally, right-to-life activists are probably inclined to exaggerate their influence, and the apparent heavy-handedness of RTLP leaders may even have hurt the right-to-life cause by helping to splinter movement leadership, by alienating fence-sitters, and by serving as a rallying point for pro-choice forces. But at the same time, politicians (though especially legislative representatives up for frequent reelection) are in many respects a skittish lot. Like birds sitting on a telephone line, they are wary of untoward movement, and they may respond whether a "threat" is real or not, at least in the short term. The reputational strategy is enhanced, then, because politics in New York are relatively competitive and because the party can offer its line.

In terms of the four possible paths or routes a party may follow in the Stage III phase posed by the model, the fourth seems most applicable; that is, the RTLP has attracted a relatively small vote percentage from the start (rarely more than 3 percent) and, as Tables 2.2 and 2.3 show, the party's electoral strength has been slowly eroding, in part at least because of party leaders' inner-directedness and obsession with issue purity. As Table 2.4 shows, the RTLP has garnered a solid core of supporters. The enrollment levels probably reflect a certain lag in support, since time will pass from the point when support grows to the point where that enhanced support reflects itself in higher enrollments. (By contrast, the 1986 enrollment levels for the Conservative and Liberal Parties were 110,485 and 62,540, respectively.) Nevertheless, it appears that enrollment levels have peaked in the low twenty-thousands.

SUMMARY

The dynamic model of party development provides an exceptionally useful format for describing, analyzing, and understanding this case of party development. Social unrest stemming from

Table 2.4
Right to Life Party Enrollment

1980	**8,031**
1981	**15,282**
1982	**15,793**
1983	**17,630**
1984	**18,933**
1985	**22,966**
1986	**21,606**

Source: New York State Board of Elections

pathbreaking changes in New York abortion law engendered controversy in New York that was soon to be felt nationwide after the Supreme Court's 1973 ruling. This unrest found expression in New York in electoral channels, aided crucially by New York's unusual electoral structure. A small, determined group of activists composed of political novices entered the electoral fray, established the RTLP, and, at least by reputation, exerted influence beyond their small numbers and limited means.

Given the four possible paths for a party proposed in Stage III of the model, its pattern of ideologically rigid inner-directedness, the party's unswerving course will continue in the fashion of a small, dogmatic organization. Though the single-minded, anti-abortion fervor of the party's adherents was central to its formation, New York's electoral system was the crucial variable in the RTLP equation. The next chapter will delve more deeply into the backgrounds and motivations of party activists and identifiers.

NOTES

1. "The Battle Over Abortion," *Time*, April 6, 1981, p. 20.
2. "Single Issue Politics," *Newsweek*, November 6, 1978, p. 48.
3. Pamela Johnston Conover and Virginia Gray, *Feminism and the New Right: Conflict over the American Family* (New York: Praeger, 1983), pp. 154–56.
4. Ibid.
5. Ibid. In their Minnesota study, they found six times as many right-to-life activists willing to vote solely on abortion, as compared with pro-choice activists. The ratio was two-to-one among Minnesota voters. Similar findings were reported in Donald Granberg, "The Abortion Activists," *Family Planning Perspectives* 13, 4 (July/August, 1981), 157–63.
6. The Alan Guttmacher Institute, *Safe and Legal: 10 Year's Experience with Legal Abortion in New York State* (New York: The Alan Guttmacher Institute, 1980).
7. Ibid., pp. 8–9
8. *Statistical Abstract of the United States*, 1985 (Washington, DC: U.S. Government Printing Office, 1985).
9. The Alan Guttmacher Institute, *Safe and Legal*, p. 7. In a 1985 telephone survey commissioned by Planned Parenthood, 79 percent of 900 New York State residents agreed that women should have the right to decide for themselves whether to obtain an abortion. Seventeen percent disagreed, and 4 percent had no opinion. See "'New Yorkers Overwhelmingly in Favor of Abortion Rights," *Cortland Standard*, December 31, 1985.
10. Ballot position is determined by gubernatorial vote. The party whose gubernatorial candidate receives the largest vote appears first on all New York ballots, followed by the other parties, according to the size of gubernatorial vote. If a party does not field a gubernatorial candidate, it forfeits the line. See State of New York Election Law, Sections 1–104, 7–116.
11. Robert Karen, "The Politics of Pressure," *The Nation*, September 20, 1975, p. 236.
12. Maurice Carroll, "State Democrats Attack Cross-Endorsement Policy," *New York Times*, January 29, 1982, p. B2. See also Milton Hoff-

man, "Major Parties Might Lose Top Ballot Positions," *Ithaca Journal*, August 26, 1982, p. 10.

13. Frank Lynn, "Conservatives and a Political Gamble in New York," *New York Times*, January 26, 1982, p. B7. See also Maurice Carroll, "Minor Party Once Again Has a Major Effect on Politics," *New York Times*, March 14, 1982, p. E7.

14. The cross-endorsement system is praised in Daniel A. Mazmanian, *Third Parties in Presidential Elections* (Washington, DC: Brookings Institution, 1974), Ch. 5, and criticized in Howard A. Scarrow, *Parties, Elections, and Representation in the State of New York* (New York: New York University Press, 1983), Ch. 3. For a summary discussion of New York's multi-party system and the RTLP, see Robert J. Spitzer, "A Political Party Is Born: Single-Issue Advocacy and the Election Law in New York State," *National Civil Review* (July/August, 1984), pp. 321–28; "The Tail Wagging the Dog: Multi-Party Politics," in *New York State Today*, ed. Peter Colby (Albany, NY: SUNY Press, 1985), pp. 61–70.

15. An excellent example of this argument can be found in Jerrold Rusk, "The Effect of the Australian Ballot Reform on Split Ticket Voting: 1876–1908," *American Political Science Review* 64 (December, 1970).

16. This discussion is summarized from Howard Scarrow's excellent *Parties, Elections, and Representation*, pp. 16, 56–59.

17. Ibid., p. 60. See also footnote 8, p. 76 in Scarrow for citations.

18. See Warren Moscow, *Politics in the Empire State* (New York: Knopf, 1948), p. 118.

19. Scarrow, *Parties, Elections, and Representation*, pp. 67–68.

20. New York minor parties, and their years of official ballot status: Prohibition (1892–1922); Socialist Labor (1896–1904); Socialist (1900–1938); Independent League (1906–1916); American (1914–1916); Farmer Labor (1920–1922); Law Preservation (1930–1934); American Labor (1936–1954); Liberal (1946–   ); Conservative (1962–   ); and Right to Life (1978–   ).

21. Karen, "The Politics of Pressure," pp. 236–37.

22. Robert A. Schoenberger, "Conservatism, Personality and Political Extremism," *American Political Science Review* (September, 1968), p. 869. See also Frank Feigert, "Conservatism, Populism, and Social Change," *American Behavioral Scientist* 17, 2 (November/December, 1973), 272–78.

23. Steven J. Rosenstone, Roy L. Behr, and Edward H. Lazarus, *Third Parties in America* (Princeton, NJ: Princeton University Press, 1984).

24. Ibid., p. 12.

25. This model was first laid out in John W. Ellwood, "A Model of the Life-Cycle of American Minor Parties," a paper presented at the 1977 Annual Meeting of the Southern Political Science Association, New Orleans, LA, November 5.

26. Neil J. Smelser, *Theory of Collective Behavior* (New York: Free Press, 1963), p. 14.

27. Michael Useem, *Protest Movements in America* (Indianapolis: Bobbs-Merrill, 1975), p. 51.

28. Other important Supreme Court cases on abortion since *Roe* include: *Planned Parenthood of Central Missouri v. Danforth* (1976), *Beal v. Doe* and *Maher v. Doe* (1977), *Poelker v. Doe* (1977), *Colautti v. Franklin* (1979), *Bellotti v. Baird* and *Hunerwald v. Baird* (1979), *Harris v. McRae* (1980), *Akron v. Akron Center for Reproductive Health* (1983), and *Thornburgh v. American College of Obstetricians and Gynecologists* (1986). The Court evidenced some retreat from *Roe* in the cases starting with *Maher*. But in the 1983 *Akron* case, the majority made it clear that *Roe* was not an aberration or a mistake, and that they have reaffirmed it "repeatedly and consistently." The three dissenters in *Akron* included the two original dissenters from *Roe*, White and Rehnquist, joined by Justice O'Connor. See Linda Greenhouse, "High Court Clears Up Any Doubts on Abortion," *New York Times*, June 19, 1983, p. E7.

In the 1986 *Thornburgh* case, the Court again strongly reaffirmed *Roe* in striking down a restrictive Pennsylvania statute. Speaking for the five-member majority, Justice Blackmun asserted, "The states are not free, under the guise of protecting maternal health or potential life, to intimidate women into continuing pregnancies." In this case, however, the dissenters to *Roe* were joined for the first time by Chief Justice Burger, who said "I agree we should re-examine Roe." Burger said that, contrary to his original expectation, the Court had extended *Roe* to require "abortion on demand." See Stuart Taylor, Jr., "Justice Uphold Abortion Rights by Narrow Vote," *New York Times*, June 12, 1986, p. A1.

29. Roger M. Williams, "The Power of Fetal Politics," reprinted in *American Politics, Policies and Priorities*, ed. Alan Shank (Boston: Allyn and Bacon, 1981), p. 178.

30. Abortion opponents differ as to how far they feel the law should go in prohibiting abortions. According to one RTLP activist interviewed, there are three levels by which one's abortion stand is measured. The first incorporates those who would allow abortions only when the life of the mother is threatened. This position is accepted by most right-to-life activists. The second level involves allowing abortions in cases of rape and incest. Activists disagree over the acceptability of this proviso. The third level encompasses those who would allow abortions when the mental health of the mother is threatened. Right-to-lifers view the latter as legal carte blanche to permit abortions on demand, and thus reject this degree of flexibility. The first two instances, however, are also often dismissed by activists as unrealistic situations, or situations

that are so rare that policy cannot be made based on such unlikely circumstances.

31. See note 3 in Chapter 3 for the list of works that focus on public opinion on abortion. A *New York Times*/CBS News Poll experimented with question wording. When asked: "do you think there should be an amendment to the Constitution prohibiting abortions, or shouldn't there be such an amendment?" 29 percent favored the proposal, and 62 percent opposed it. But when asked: "Do you believe that there should be an amendment to the Constitution protecting the life of the unborn child, or shouldn't there be such an amendment?" the responses were 50 percent in favor and 39 percent opposed. See E. J. Dionne, Jr., "Abortion Poll: Not Clear-Cut," *New York Times*, August 18, 1980. Despite ambiguity in polling results and interpretations, none of the right-to-life literature examined cited public opinion to buttress its views. A 1981 *Washington Post*/ABC News poll reported that 54 percent of those surveyed opposed federal funding of abortion for poor women, through this result says nothing about abortions when the government is not footing the bill.

32. The Alan Guttmacher Institute, *Safe and Legal*, p. 7; Frederick S. Jaffe, Barbara L. Lindheim, and Philip R. Lee, *Abortion Politics: Private Morality and Public Policy* (New York: McGraw-Hill, 1981), Ch. 8.

33. Ibid., pp. 99–101.

34. These factors are summarized in Pam Conover, Steve Coombs, and Virginia Gray, "the Attitudinal Roots of Single-Issue Politics: The Case of 'Women's Issues,' " a paper presented at the 1980 Annual Meeting of the American Political Science Association, The Washington Hilton Hotel, Washington, DC, August 28–31.

35. Ibid., p. 30.

36. E. J. Dionne, Jr., "Candidates Talk to the Issues, But Address Their Supporters," *New York Times*, September 28, 1980.

37. See, for example, Michael Margolis and Kevin Neary, "Pressure Politics Revisited: The Anti-Abortion Campaign," *Policy Studies Journal* (Spring, 1980), p. 703.

38. "Abortion Clinic and 2 Doctors' Offices in Pensacola, Fla., Bombed," *New York Times*, December 26, 1984.

39. Dudley Clendinen, "Abortion Clinic Bombings Have Caused Disruption for Many," *New York Times*, February 6, 1985.

40. "The Battle Over Abortion," p. 21.

41. The state legislature reversed itself in 1972, but Governor Rockefeller vetoed the more restrictive new law. No attempt to change the New York law has succeeded since then.

42. For example, see Philip Converse, "The Nature of Belief Systems

in Mass Publics," in *Ideology and Discontent*, ed. David Apter (New York: Free Press, 1964); Sidney Verba and Norman Nie, *Participation in America* (New York: Harper and Row, 1972); John W. Ellwood and Robert J. Spitzer, "The Democratic National Telethons," *Journal of Politics* 41, 3 (August, 1979), 828–64.

43. The same pattern was found in Sagar C. Jain and Laurel F. Gooch, *Georgia Abortion Act 1968* (Chapel Hill, NC: University of North Carolina, School of Public Health, 1972), pp. 35–37; also, Kristin Luker, *Abortion and the Politics of Motherhood* (Berkeley, CA: University of California Press, 1984), Ch. 6.

44. Frank Smallwood, *The Other Candidates* (Hanover, NH: University Press of New England, 1983), p. 196.

45. George Vecsey, "Antiabortion Candidate Sparks Funding Debate," *New York Times*, February 9, 1976.

46. Herbert E. Alexander, *Financing the 1976 Election* (Washington, DC: Congressional Quarterly Press, 1979), pp. 205, 209–11.

47. Polls indicated that abortion played a minor role in vote decisions. For example, a *New York Times*/CBS Poll of Massachusetts Democrats on primary day indicated that only 7 percent of those surveyed considered abortion an important issue, and less than half of them voted for McCormack (she received about 3.5 percent of the vote). Carl E. Schneider and Maris A. Vinovskis, eds., *The Law and Politics of Abortion* (Lexington, MA: Lexington Books, 1980), p. 193.

48. Christopher Lydon, "Abortion Foe Has Solid Core of Support," *New York Times*, March 2, 1976.

49. Smallwood, *The Other Candidates*, p. 205.

50. One party official proposed that the party nominate Jesse Jackson, based on his right-to-life sentiments, with the hope that this would draw votes away from Carter. But there was little support for this move from either Jackson or the party.

51. "Right-to-Life Party Doubles Enrollment," *Cortland Standard*, November 3, 1984. See also, "State Right to Life Party Won't Nominate Presidential Candidate," *Ithaca Journal*, September 9, 1984.

52. Republican platforms in 1976, 1980, and 1984 called for a constitutional amendment to "restore protection of the right to life for the unborn child" (from the 1980 platform). The platforms also supported efforts to prevent use of taxpayer dollars for abortion. The 1980 and 1984 Democratic platforms affirmed support for the Supreme Court's decision in *Roe*, and the 1984 platform explicitly stated its support for "reproductive freedom," to be protected against government restrictions or interference.

53. Despite a Catholic background, the incumbent Democrat in 1978,

Hugh Carey, consistently supported the pro-choice position, including Medicaid funding. Possibly in response to political pressure, he did announce his support for a bill requiring doctors in some instances to inform a minor's parents before performing an abortion (although, to the present time, this measure has not been enacted). See Robin Herman, "Carey May Back Abortions Rule on Notification," *New York Times*, March 25, 1981. The 1978 Republican challenger, Perry Duryea, modified his stand on abortion to bring it more closely in line with the RTLP view. But he was equivocal during the campaign, and the RTLP did not forgive him for his key role as a Rockefeller protégé in enacting the 1970 law.

54. See Steve Geimann, "Right-to-Life Party Lost Ground," *Ithaca Journal*, November 4, 1982; Joseph Galu, "Right-to-Life Vote Falls in Final Tallies," *Utica Observer-Dispatch*, December 3, 1982.

55. Many of those I interviewed purposefully identified themselves as single-issue activists. From the start, McCormack has trumpeted the single-issue label. See Phyllis Bernstein, "Anti-Abortion Candidate for President," *New York Times*, November 30, 1975.

56. This finding is consistent with what is known about other right-to-life activists, despite the fact that Catholics as a whole are only slightly less supportive of the pro-choice view than non-Catholics. See Margolis and Neary, "Pressure Politics Revisited," pp. 704–5. Occupationally, RTLP leaders are what might be labeled petit bourgeois. Their occupations include school teacher, farmer, security guard, small businessman, and housewife.

57. An example of this at the national level was seen in the resignation of three staunchly pro-life congressmen from an advisory board of the National Pro-Life PAC, over the committee's decision to target nine pro-choice members of Congress for defeat. See *New York Times*, June 4, 1981. Intra-movement splits continue to plague the right-to-life movement at all levels. See Tim Miller, "Two Competing 'Pro-Life' Measures Split the Anti-Abortion Lobby," *National Journal*, March 20, 1982, pp. 511–13; Sheila Caudle, "Weakened by In-fighting, Right-to-Lifers Talk of Unity," *Ithaca Journal*, December 13, 1982.

58. Ironically, Nicolosi was defeated in his 1980 re-election bid by a Republican with Conservative and RTLP endorsements. Nicolosi's narrow margin of loss was smaller than his opponent's vote on the RTLP line. Mary Fiess, "Right-to-Life Party Is Losing Friends, not Influencing People," *Ithaca Journal*, May 29, 1980.

59. Ibid.

60. Patricia Braus, "Lobbyist Says Right-to-Life Endorsement is an 'Albatross,' " *Ithaca Journal*, October 14, 1982.

61. The National Pro-Life PAC criticized McCormack as a "purist [who is] holding up unreasonable and impractical standards." RTLP officials argued that the McCormack candidacy in 1980 would be useful as a vehicle for dramatizing the abortion issue, whereas Reagan's abortion position would be lost in the larger context of his candidacy. Frank Lynn, "Anti-Abortion Groups Split on Reagan's Candidacy," *New York Times*, June 22, 1980.

62. In the aftermath of this agreement, McCormack said: "All the Democrats' Right to Life Party endorsements are in jeopardy." Richard Meislin, "Abortion Foes Issue Warning to a Legislator," *New York Times*, May 18, 1980.

63. For example, Timothy Noah, "The Right-to-Life Split," *The New Republic*, March 21, 1981, pp. 7–9.

64. See Schoenberger, "Conservatism, Personality, and Political Extremism"; and Feigert, "Conservatism, Populism, and Social Change."

65. The Hyde Amendment is discussed in Joyce Gelb and Marian L. Palley, "Women and Interest Group Politics: A Comparative Analysis of Federal Decision-Making," *Journal of Politics* (May, 1979), pp. 362–92; and Schneider and Vinovskis, *The Law and Politics of Abortion*, Ch. 7.

66. See Joseph Califano, *Governing America* (New York: Simon and Schuster, 1981).

67. Margolis and Neary, "Pressure Politics Revisited," pp. 705–7.

3

ACTIVISTS AND IDENTIFIERS

The overall political antecedents, processes, and consequences of abortion have been the subject of wide-ranging description and analysis.[1] Much of this literature, admittedly, has been polemical in nature.[2] Some aspects of the abortion issue have been exhaustively studied, such as the nature of public opinion on abortion.[3] Other aspects are less well understood, such as the motivational bases and nature of the activists and leaders caught up in the abortion movement; however, some provocative research has been done in this area.[4] Most of these studies examine small groups of New Right (including abortion-related) activists.

Aside from learning more about New York's Right to Life Party, an analysis of party leaders and identifiers provides a singular opportunity to examine both right-to-life activists—as identified by their willingness to serve in leadership positions within the party—and right-to-life identifiers—citizens without a history of activism (we assume) who have nevertheless indicated, at the level of voting, their commitment to the right-to-life movement. Voter enrollment is *prima facie* evidence of a willingness to vote (and therefore express an overt political commitment) on the basis of a single issue. Thus, the analysis begins with a clearly identified group (predicated on the identifiable behavior of party enrollment) of single-issue voters and activists. Given this base, what are the dispositions and orientations of these right-to-lifers? How do the party leaders compare with the identifiers? What motivates both groups to involve themselves with a small, new minor party? How do they compare with other right-to-life groups? What does this imply for electoral politics as an arena for political action, as compared to the realm of lobbying and interest group activity? And how does this relate to the larger realm of single-issue politics of the 1970s and 1980s? This study can provide a unique perspective on these questions, since existing studies focus either on small groups of activists or on those subgroups in nationwide public opinion studies that respond strongly to abortion-related questions. Those enrolled in the RTLP, however, are defined by their *behavior* (as are the activists). Thus, this exploration of a minor party, based on a behaviorally defined single-issue group will help to serve the larger purpose of establishing analytic connections between mass discontent, institutional structures and concrete political action.

RIGHT-TO-LIFE ACTIVISM

Several previous studies have attempted to examine aspects of single-issue social movement activism, focusing primarily on motivations and bases of support. A study of anti-ERA lobbyists in Texas concluded that its adherents shared conservative political attitudes (mistrust of big government, belief in the communist threat, etc.), were concerned about the state of contemporary morality, shared strong religious beliefs, shared a certain small town provincialism, but at the same time registered high levels of political efficacy, prior participation in politics, and education.[5]

A study that focused its attention more generally on the New Right observed in particular that right-to-life support was tied to conservative or traditional attitudes toward sex roles, the status of women in society, and personal morality.[6] In general, they observed support for the New Right to be tied closely to political conservatism, religious fundamentalism, and middle socio-economic status.[7] A study focusing exclusively on abortion activists also observed high religiosity, adherence to traditional moral values, and political conservatism.[8] Another study by this same researcher, which analyzed factors associated with generalized opposition to abortion, found that conservatism in personal morality was the most potent explanatory factor (along with religious affiliation), above class status/education, generalized anti-killing attitudes, political conservatism, and attitudes about the women's liberation movement.[9] Sociologist Kristin Luker offered this composite portrait of the typical female right-to-life activist in California:

The average pro-life woman is . . . a forty-four-year-old married woman who grew up in a large metropolitan area. She married at age seventeen and has three children or more. Her father was a high school graduate, and she has some college education or may have a B.A. degree. She is not employed in the paid work force and is married to a small businessman or a lower-level white-collar worker; her family income is $30,000 a year. She is catholic (and may have converted) and her religion is one of the most important aspects of her life: she attends church at least once a week and occasionally more often.[10]

It is clear that we find much conservative coherence spanning political, religious/moral, and social dimensions when dealing with the New Right generally and abortion specifically. This coherence is even greater among the activists in these movements.

Before proceeding with the analysis, some clarification of the nature of activism is appropriate. Most importantly, it is well established that those who are more active in politics are generally not representative of larger populations. This holds true for both attitudinal and demographic characteristics.[11] The primary lines of cleavage fall between those who do not vote or otherwise participate, those who participate solely through the act of voting, and those who participate beyond the act of voting (activists). With this in mind, I hypothesized that the Right to Life Party (RTLP) sample—not including the identifiers—would closely parallel the patterns found among other New Right activists, despite geographical and temporal differences. Given the relatively small number of RTLP adherents in New York (18,933 enrolled RTLP voters in 1984), it seemed likely that the nonactivist identifiers would share the activists' moral/religious perspectives, but lack the same level of political coherence, awareness, participation, and socio-economic background.

THE RTLP SAMPLE

In the Summer and Fall of 1983, I conducted a mail survey of RTLP leaders and identifiers. Nine hundred thirty-two identifiers and all of the one hundred party leaders were sent survey questionnaires (See Appendix 1 for sample questionnaire). Of these, 32 leaders (32 percent) and 217 identifiers (23 percent) responded after two mail appeals.[12] Admittedly, the return rate falls below the desired 50–percent response rate; however, several considerations serve to enhance confidence in the reliability of this sample. First, the relatively small, homogeneous nature of the universe enhances confidence in a sample that does not reach the 50–percent mark. Second, most similar studies have relied on even smaller samples of a more amorphous, vaguely defined universe.[13] Yet, their findings have demonstrated an analytic consistency pertinent to this study. Finally, some brief comparisons between the activists in this study and a 1980 survey of members of the National Right-to-Life Committee (NRLC) reveal considerable consistency. For example, among respondents in the 1980 study, 90 percent had at least some college education, compared to almost 85 percent among RTLP leaders. Seventy-five percent of the RTLP leaders are married, compared to 87 percent in the NRLC study; 86 percent of the NRLC sample attend church at least weekly, compared to 84 percent of the RTLP leaders.[14] Considering the evident differences between the NRLC nationwide sample and the New York RTLP activists, the observed similarities lend added credence to the reliability of this sample.

Demographic profile

The RTLP sample reveals some expected demographic characteristics, but also some unexpected ones. (Results cited refer to the entire sample. Where a significant divergence between leaders and identifiers occurs, it will be noted.) As expected, most of the sample are married (65 percent), with a higher rate (75 percent) among leaders. Fifty-five percent of the sample are females, but 53 percent of leaders are male. Controlling for other factors, the only significant sex-related divergences found were education and efficacy; in both instances, men had more. The median age of the sample is relatively young (33), with the median age of the leadership somewhat higher (39). This age pattern parallels the conventional wisdom that younger age cohorts are less strongly tied to the existing political order, and therefore more subject to conversion to a new party. The vast majority of the sample are lifelong state residents, clearly indicating the indigenous nature of the party from top to bottom.

Not surprisingly, education levels differ between leaders and followers. Among the former, 53 percent are college graduates, compared with 38 percent of the latter. (In the 1980 NRLC survey, 58 percent were college graduates.) The average number of children for the RTLP sample was 2.2, compared to 3.4 in the NRLC study. When broken down by age, those 46 to 64 averaged 4.1 children, followed by 31 to 45 (2.8), 65 to 82 (2.5) and 18 to 30 (0.8). The breakdown for the NRLC sample was roughly one child more in each category.

Occupationally, professional-technical workers composed 23 percent of the sample, followed by 22 percent housewives. The one divergence between leaders and identifiers was in the self-employed category, where 28 percent of leaders fell, compared with only 7 percent of identifiers. Clearly, self-employment would allow for greater work-schedule flexibility, thereby making activism easier. Finally, income figures show that almost half of the sample earn over $25,000 per year—the figure slightly higher for leaders—closely parallel to Luker's study.[15]

Religion

Consistent with the religious predilections of other right-to-life groups, most RTLP members are Catholics—specifically, 71 percent of identifiers, and 84 percent of leaders. (Luker's study reported 80 percent Catholicism.) Of the remainder, most of the rest are Protestant. Of the 36 respondents who labeled themselves Protestant (15 percent), 30 were members of fundamentalist sects that other research shows share right-to-life concerns in nearly the same degree as Catholics.[16] Despite this, Catholics were more likely to take an uncompromising view of abortion than Protestants. Among Catholics, 49 percent said that abortions should never be allowed, compared with 33 percent of Protestants. At the same time, Catholics reported greater frequency of church attendance than Protestants (79 percent of Catholics report going every week, compared to 51 percent of Protestants).

In terms of religiosity, 84 percent of leaders and 68 percent of identifiers report attending church "every week." (The figure was 63 percent in Luker's study.) The percents reporting church attendance "almost every week" are 10 percent and 13 percent, respectively. One indication of the potency of religiosity is found when it is crossed with vote recollections. Among those who reported having voted for Ellen McCormack for president in 1980, 84 percent attend church weekly; of those who voted for Reagan, 80 percent attend church weekly; for Carter supporters, the figure is 54 percent, and for Anderson, it is 29 percent. Religiosity is also highly and directly related to participation in abortion protest activity (gamma = .62), and to more stern attitudes about abortion (gamma = .48). It bears no strong relationship, however, to attitudes about traditional sex roles. In terms of evaluations of political leaders, religiosity is strongly related to approval of New York Senator Alphonse D'Amato, and very strongly related to disapproval of U.S. Senator Edward Kennedy. In general, the preference rankings controlling for religiosity parallel closely the overall rankings summarized in Table 3.6. Here, one may reasonably presume, lies the moral imperative that propels RTLP activity. The overriding importance of religion is endorsed by the finding that there is no particular relation between frequency of church attendance and education (gamma = .07) or income (gamma = .16).[17]

Partisanship and political participation

One key question to be addressed concerning RTLP members is prior party affiliation, if any. Were they drawn primarily from the ranks of the disaffected (i.e., non-voters), or were they drawn primarily from the major parties? If so, are there more converted Democrats or Republicans?

As Table 3.1 shows, RTLP members were most likely to be former Democrats, though this is much more true among lead-

Table 3.1
Previous Party Identification

	Leaders	Identifiers
Democrat	41%	28%
Republican	34	21
Conservative	3	11
Liberal	3	2
Independent	6	10
Not Enrolled	12	27
	99% (32)	99% (193)

Variations from 100% due to rounding error.

Table 3.2
When Should Abortions Be Allowed?

	Leaders	Identifiers
Never	53%	42%
Mother's life at stake	44	28
Mother's life, rape, incest	0	23
If mother has difficulty caring for child	0	1
Conscience and judgment of woman	0	3
Other	3	3
	100% (32)	100% (197)

ers. Indeed, my interviews with top party leaders showed nearly all of them to be former Democrats. (Recall that RTLP leader Ellen McCormack's initial foray into national politics involved entrance in the Democratic Party's 1976 presidential primaries.) The other main difference between leaders and identifiers is the larger proportion of identifiers drawn from those previously unenrolled. Still, RTLP members are primarily converts from other parties rather than the formerly uninvolved.

Differences between leaders and identifiers became more pronounced when both were asked to recall their prior voting patterns in 1980 and 1982 (understanding the limitations of recalled voting data). In the presidential race, 66 percent of the leaders reported having voted for McCormack for president in 1980, compared with 17 percent of followers. Reagan support was reported as 22 percent for leaders and 43 percent for followers. Similarly, 84 percent of leaders reported having supported Robert Bohner as the RTLP gubernatorial candidate, compared with 25 percent of identifiers. If these figures are close to the actual rate of voting, they indicate a serious problem for the party, since its continued existence is predicated on its gubernatorial candidate receiving at least 50,000 votes—the minimum needed for official recognition (Bohner received 52,356 votes in 1982). Despite the unreliability of recall data, it is clear that a considerable disparity exists between leaders and followers in support of these RTLP candidates. This fact takes on added significance when one realizes that, when voters recall how they voted, after the fact, they tend to report having voted for the winner in numbers that exceed the actual vote totals. In terms of loyalty to right-to-life principles across the entire sample, those who had voted for RTLP candidates were more strongly opposed to abortion than those who had supported major-party candidates.

Greater loyalty to the RTLP by the leaders was also exhibited when respondents were asked whether they preferred to vote for candidates running solely on the RTLP line, or for major-party candidates jointly endorsed by the RTLP. Among leaders, 61 percent preferred voting for RTLP-only candidates, compared with 44 percent of the identifiers. The fact that reported leader support is not even higher might be explained by the fact that RTLP leaders previously interviewed indicated a preference for an electoral strategy of major party-RTLP joint endorsements. As discussed in the last chapter, the RTLP does better at the polls on its own line when it endorses a major-party candidate (that is, garners more votes on the RTLP line), instead of simply running its own people without other endorsements.

If RTLP members are disenchanted with the major parties, they share clear perceptions of where the major parties stand on abortion. Ninety-seven percent of leaders, and 80 percent of identifiers reported that the Republican Party was closer to the right-to-life position than the Democrats. Not surprisingly, the more educated the RTLP members, the more likely they are to perceive this as true. The fact that the plurality of party members were former Democrats has clearly not intervened to produce impressions of the Democratic Party as closer to their liking.

Insofar as attitudes about abortion are the keystone of this party, the data in Table 3.2 show in particular party leaders' stern attitudes; more than half could conceive of no circumstances whatsoever under which abortions should be permitted. Even among the identifiers, this figure was more than four out of ten. These attitudes were also held consistently across education levels.

This stern attitude toward abortion is also carried into daily experience. When asked whether they ever talked about abortion at home, work, church, socially, other, or almost never (allowing for multiple responses), only 13 respondents (5 percent) in the entire sample responded "almost never." Identifiers reported an average of three of the possible circumstances, and leaders an average of three-and-a-half.

If most RTLP members take the "conservative" position on abortion, they do not consider it so in reporting their overall ideological predilection. More identifiers, surprisingly, consider themselves conservatives (40 percent) than leaders (34 percent), yet the largest response in both groups is "moderate" (see Table 3.3).

The survey posed two open-ended questions. The first asked respondents why they enrolled in the RTLP. The most frequent response for both leaders and identifiers was some kind of statement about the wrongness of abortion, variously mentioning its immorality, that they felt it to be murder, that it violated religious and/or moral codes. Identifiers, however, were more likely to respond in this fashion (69 percent) than the leaders (45 percent). Leaders were more likely to emphasize political consequences or motivations, dissatisfaction with the major parties, and the desire to influence others on the issue.

Respondents were also asked how they thought the RTLP could best promote the right-to-life objective. The most frequent responses for both groups were: first, through education and information campaigns, and second, through work in the electoral process. Even for leaders, then, greater emphasis is placed on issue advocacy than concrete political tactics and strategic/organizational skills. This result is consonant with a party structure that strives foremost for issue purity, rather than more mainstream bargaining. As mentioned, the RTLP has followed an inner-directed strategy based on devotion to the ending of abortions, at the expense of expanding its base or gaining greater legitimacy, even among other components of the right-to-life movement. This illustrates the nature of the RTLP-as-social-movement. As Conover and Gray observed, "issues are the language through which social movements organize and take action."[18]

Activism

To observe that party leaders exhibit greater activism than identifiers is to state the obvious. What is of interest, however, is the degree of activism of both, and in particular the activism level, if any, of the identifiers.

For example, 91 percent of the leaders report having written a letter to a newspaper or public official about abortion; but 42 percent of the identifiers reported the same. About 94 percent of leaders have engaged in activities to protest abortion, like signing petitions, attending meetings, etc. The rate for identifiers is 75 percent. This is a clear indication of the grassroots phenomenon.

The gap between the two becomes much wider when other direct political action is considered. When asked if they belonged to other political groups or organizations, including other right-to-life groups, only 23 percent of the identifiers responded "yes," compared to 78 percent of the leaders.

Table 3.4 also illustrates the marked differences in activism. More than two-thirds of the leaders engage in four political acts beyond voting, compared with only 13 percent of identifiers. When we control for education, only mild differences appear. For example, 16 percent of those with high school educations reported the highest level of activism, compared with 24 percent for those who have attended college. Among those who reported that they had engaged in abortion protest activity, education levels had no effect. Income level is also related to activism (since the rich can more easily afford to make time for political work), but again, the degree of difference is only slightly more than for education, and the gap is found almost entirely among party leaders. That is, income levels have virtually no effect on identifier activism, but a moderate effect for the leader sample.

Evaluations of political figures, organizations, issues

Survey respondents were asked to evaluate a variety of issues and political figures to gauge the breadth of their ideological consistency. Among this sample, we would expect to find the kind of ideological consistency found in other similar surveys.

Three questions were asked to tap into respondent perceptions about sex roles. As Table 3.5 shows, the respondents contradict the expectation that this group would share traditional sex role attitudes. But when sex-role attitudes are crossed with attitudes toward abortion, we do find a direct correlation in traditional attitudes. For example, among those holding no traditional sex-role attitudes ("None" in Table 3.5), 34 percent feel abortions should "never" be allowed. Among those holding all traditional attitudes ("3" in Table 3.5), 72 percent respond "never" to the abortion question. Thus, within the generally hard line on abortion maintained by the RTLP sample, we still find variance in degree related to sex-role attitudes. By contrast, sex-role attitudes have no strong correlation with levels of education or income. Nor is there any clear relationship between sex-role attitudes and religiosity.

Table 3.3
Do You Consider Yourself a:

	Leaders	Identifiers
Liberal	9%	7%
Conservative	34	40
Moderate	47	42
Other (Christian)[*]	9	11
	99% (32)	100% (191)

[*]Most responses in the "other" category were "Christian."
Variations from 100% due to rounding error.

Table 3.4
Percentage Distribution of Number of Political Acts Beyond Voting

	None	1	2	3	4	Total
Leaders	0%	0	12	16	72	100% (32)
Identifiers	33%	29	16	9	13	100% (198)

The four political acts are: wearing campaign buttons, etc.;
attending political meetings; working for a candidate; and,
contributing money. Questions drawn from CPS American
National Election Study Survey.

Table 3.5
Percentage Distribution of Number of Traditional Sex Role Responses

	(no traditional responses) None	1	2	(all traditional responses) 3	Total
Leaders	50%	28	19	3	100% (32)
Identifiers	51%	26	16	7	100% (198)

ªThe three questions asked which response respondents agreed with: 1) In general men are more qualified than women for jobs that have great responsibility; or 2) many qualified women can't get good jobs; men with the same skills have much less trouble. 1) It's more natural for men to have the top responsible jobs in the country; or 2) set discrimination keeps women from the top jobs. 1) By nature, women are happiest when they are making a home and caring for children; or 2) our society, not nature, teaches women to prefer homemaking to work outside the home. Questions drawn from the CPS American Nation Election Study Survey.

While working with the original questionnaires, I noticed pervasive dissatisfaction with these three questions, especially among the leaders. Respondents felt the questions posed simplistic and unsatisfactory choices. Were I asked to respond, I would share these sentiments. Nevertheless, the questions were used for the sake of uniformity and comparability.

The mean scores in Table 3.6 also reveal some unexpected evaluations. The top five most positive mean evaluations (1.0 = most positive, 3.0 = neutral, 5.0 = most negative) correctly identify the five closest allies of the right-to-life movement, and the rank order for leaders and identifiers is nearly identical. Senator D'Amato was elected in 1980 with the active support and endorsement of the RTLP, and it is likely that leaders would be more aware of this than identifiers. Mean support for the death penalty parallels generalized conservatism—though the death penalty is favored by most New Yorkers. Yet support for the death penalty is not as pronounced as one might expect. Almost half of the leaders (48 percent) expressed a negative evaluation of having a death penalty in New York, compared with 34 percent of identifiers. This is surprising both for its size and as evidence of greater leader support for the liberal position. Moreover, controlling for education has no effect on the trends.

The evaluation of the Equal Rights Amendment (ERA) also reveals a disjunction between leaders and identifiers. Among the former, only 9 percent indicated positive feelings for the

Table 3.6
Mean Evaluations of Political Figures, Issues[a]

	Combined	Leaders	Identifiers
Phyllis Schlafly	2.29	1.90	2.44
Ronald Reagan	2.40	2.19	2.42
Moral Majority	2.44	2.19	2.46
Alphonse D'Amato	2.47	2.12	2.58
Jerry Falwell	2.77	2.28	2.95
having death penalty	2.88	3.19	2.78
George Bush	3.08	3.48	2.95
Henry Kissinger	3.16	3.32	3.11
Jimmy Carter	3.31	4.17	3.15
Supreme Court	3.42	4.37	3.19
Equal Rights Amendment	3.48	4.41	3.24
Mario Cuomo	3.49	4.31	3.29
James Watt	3.54	3.36	3.57
Thomas P. "Tip" O'Neill	3.54	4.37	3.32
National Rifle Association	3.62	3.81	3.54
Walter Mondale	3.75	4.53	3.55
George Wallace	3.81	3.90	3.78
Daniel P. Moynihan	3.84	4.62	3.62
Richard Nixon	3.86	3.87	3.83
Edward Kennedy	4.00	4.62	3.87
N[s]	(249)[b]	(32)	(198)

[a] Respondents were given a five-point scale: 1 = very positive, 2 = somewhat positive, 3 = neutral, 4 = slightly negative, 5 = very negative.

[b] The 19 cases not included in the "combined" sample are respondents that did not indicate information revealing whether they were leaders or not.

ERA, compared to 38 percent of the latter. In the 1980 NRLC survey, the percent who registered approval of the ERA was also 9 percent. Also, the overall negative evaluation of the National Rifle Association (NRA) was unexpected. Contrary to the expectation of greater leader conservatism, leaders expressed greater negative feelings than identifiers. Controlling for education level had no appreciable effect on these results. When we control for upstate-downstate differences, we find more support for the NRA upstate; but even upstate, more respondents hold negative than positive feelings.

The last five political figures on the list have the most negative ratings for the combined sample. But when leader and identifier rankings are examined separately, we see that Wallace and Nixon (the two traditional conservatives) are rated more highly by the leaders, though not by the identifiers.

To further clarify the nature of these support patterns, the 20 evaluations were crossed with former party identification to determine if RTLP members were bringing prior loyalties with them in their evaluations. The results, however, indicate not. For example, former Democrats rated Moynihan and Tip O'Neill more positively than former Republicans (comparing percent of positive responses), but the Democrats also rated Reagan more positively and Mondale less positively. The differences between former Republicans and Democrats seemed almost random, in fact.

When religious preference was crossed with the evaluations, no clear patterns or differences emerged, with two interesting exceptions. Catholics shared a relatively low evaluation of Jimmy Carter (22 percent positive), compared with a much higher Protestant rating (40 percent positive). Second, evaluations of D'Amato also varied significantly by religion. Catholics rated him 66 percent positively (D'Amato is a Catholic), compared with only 33 percent of Protestants giving a positive evaluation. Catholic suspicion of a southern fundamentalist seems to linger, as does Protestant suspicion of a native Catholic.

Finally, respondents enforce the inference that political awareness of candidates and issues is relatively high by reporting high attention to the news. As Table 3.7 shows, self-reported awareness of news is considerable even for identifiers.

Table 3.7
Do You Follow Government and Public Affairs:

	Leaders	Identifiers
Most of the time	72%	50%
Some of the time	28	36
Only now and then	0	8
Hardly at all	0	6
	100%	100%
	(32)	(197)

Question drawn from CPS American National Election Study Survey.

Political efficacy and trust in government

In their study of anti-ERA activists in Texas, Brady and Tedin observed a high degree of participation and efficacy among their sample.[19] This finding parallels the RTLP sample. Responses to four standard efficacy questions are compared in Table 3.8. In all instances, RTLP leaders exceed the high levels of efficacy observed by Brady and Tedin. Surprisingly, RTLP identifiers exceed the anti-ERA activists in efficacy for two of the four questions. There can be no doubt that this factor alone sets RTLP identifiers apart from any traditional group of party identifiers, and is an added indication of the motivational force at the grassroots of the abortion issue. Table 3.9 scales low efficacy responses to the four efficacy questions, still indicating leaders' high efficacy, followed to a lesser degree by identifiers. Again, the most important observation to be noted is not derived from the lead-

Table 3.8

A Comparison of Responses to Political Efficacy[a]

	Brady & Tedin 1975[b]	RTLP Leaders	RTLP Identifiers
People like me don't have any say about what the government does.			
Agree	18%	0%	27%
Disagree	75	100	66
No opinion/undecided	07	0	7
	100%	100%	100%
	(154)	(32)	(198)
Voting is the only way people like me have any say about how the government runs things.			
Agree	26%	34%	42%
Disagree	63	66	53
No opinion/undecided	11	0	4
	100%	100%	99%
	(154)	(32)	(198)
Sometimes politics and government seem so complicated that a person like me can't really understand what's going on.			
Agree	55%	32%	48%
Disagree	40	68	45
No opinion/undecided	5	0	6
	100%	100%	99%
	(154)	(32)	(198)
I don't think public officials care much what people like me think.			
Agree	42%	26%	42%
Disagree	46	74	51
No opinion/undecided	12	0	6
	100%	100%	99%
	(154)	(32)	(198)

[a]Question wording from CPS American National Election Study Survey.

[b]Data taken from: David W. Brady and Kent L. Tedin, "Ladies in Pink," Social Science Quarterly, March, 1976, p. 573. Based on interviews with anti-ERA Activists in Texas.

Variations from 100% due to rounding error.

Table 3.9
Percentage Distribution of Number of Low Efficacy Responses[a]

	(high efficacy) None	1	2	3	(low efficacy) 4	Total
Leaders	28%	56	12	3	0	99%
Identifiers	25	27	23	16	10	101%

[a] For question wording, see Table 8.
Variations from 100% due to rounding error.

Table 3.10
Percentage Distribution of Cynicism Trust in Government Responses[a]

	(Low cynicism) 4	5	6	7	8	9	(High cynicism) 10	11	12	Total
Leaders	0%	0	0	10	0	35	40	15	0	100% (20)
Identifiers	1%	0	4	3	7	16	24	39	6	100% (153)

[a] Responses to four questions were scaled to produce the above distribution. The four questions were: Do you think that people in government waste a lot of money we pay in taxes, waste some of it, or not very much? 1. not much 2. some 3. a lot 4. no opinion. How much time do you think you can trust the government in Washington to do what is right? 1. always 2. most of the time 3. some of the time 4. never. Would you say that the government is pretty much run by a few big interests looking out for themselves or that it is run for the benefit of all the people? 1. for benefit of all 2. few big interests 3. no opinion. Do you think that quite a few of the people running the government are crooked, not very many, or hardly any? 1. hardly any 2. not many 3. quite a few. Questions drawn from CPS American National Election Study Survey.

ers' scores, since we know them to be activists in other realms. Rather, it is the response of the identifiers, who by and large have no prior history of political activism. Despite generally high efficacy, Table 3.10 reveals low trust/ high cynicism toward the government. Cynicism is more pronounced among identifiers, but neither part of the sample shares anything resembling confidence in the ability of government to get things done. This is also true when we control for education. This series of questions is one benchmark of the changing nature of activism. Traditionally, persons registering high efficacy would also be likely to register relatively high levels of trust in government. Today, the norm has obviously shifted, to the point that it centers on the degree of negative attitudes toward government, rather than whether such attitudes are present.

Upstate-downstate differences

Insofar as the RTLP is a creature of New York politics, one added important factor requires exploration—namely, upstate-downstate differences. Like states such as California, Illinois, and Florida, New York politics continue to split geographically. This characteristic was illustrated in 1982 when Democrat Mario Cuomo was elected governor by carrying only nine of the state's 62 countries—the five counties of New York City, two other downstate counties, and only two upstate counties (Erie, which includes Buffalo, and Albany County, which includes the state capital).

Consistent with Republican strength upstate and Democratic strength downstate, more former Republicans are to be found upstate, and more former Conservatives (most, in fact) downstate.[20] In general, slightly more support is evidenced by RTLP members for Democratic candidates downstate, and Republican candidates upstate, as judged by responses to questions about RTLP voting in the previous presidential and gubernatorial elections.

On the other hand, no significant upstate-downstate differences were observed when respondents were asked which of the major parties was closer to the right-to-life position. Eighty percent of upstaters and 84 percent of downstaters both said that the Republican Party was more sympathetic. Questions relating to RTLP activism and support generally revealed slightly higher levels downstate, attributable primarily to the fact that the party was born downstate and is led mostly by downstaters. Among the other factors considered, only one evidenced a significant upstate-downstate split. In giving their reactions to the NRA, downstate residents gave a 14 percent positive rating, compared to a 35 percent positive rating by upstaters. The obvious explanation lies in the fact that in the more rural upstate region, gun possession and use for hunting and recreation is more of a way of life.

SUMMARY

The New York RTLP sample evidences many basic similarities in comparison to other studies of New Right groups—especially demographic characteristics, and the overriding importance of religiosity. These findings are important in and of themselves, to the extent that they add to the corpus of data on these contemporary political/social movements. The relatively high levels of political awareness, concern and efficacy are consistent with the conventional wisdom about activists and activism. The RTLP activist sample, however, did not show an automatic adherence to conservatism across the board. In fact, one might posit that the most appropriate "plane of consistency" is not traditional conservatism for the RTLP activists, but the right-to-life dimension itself. The right-to-life issue has indeed become the ideology, to the extent that evaluations of issues, candidates, and the like link almost solely to that issue. On its face, this observation might seem to be simply another definition of single-issue politics, and therefore a statement that is true about RTLP activists by definition. But this misses the point; namely, that most studies of New Right groups assume, if not demonstrate, a broader conservative ideological component—even if it is only limited to social conservatism. The findings here, however, suggest that even the social conservative plane is not as pervasive for this sample. For these right-to-lifers, abortion is the ideology.

The absence of consistent, strong traditional sex-role values among the RTLP sample might seem on its face to contradict

Luker's study (and others) that emphasize this as one, if not the central, dimension underlying the abortion debate. As Luker says, "this round of the abortion debate is so passionate and hard-fought *because it is a referendum on the place and meaning of motherhood.*"[21] She finds that "feminists" and "housewives" split sharply in their world views, including their views of the nature and meaning of motherhood, and therefore on the issue of abortion.[22] My findings do not contradict this perspective; in fact, they show a direct relation between traditional sex-role attitudes and strong feelings against abortion. But what the results also show is that there are a great many in the RTLP who do not share these traditional attitudes about sex roles. One may reasonably conclude, then, that traditional sex-role attitudes are likely to yield opposition to abortion; but opposition to abortion does not necessarily signal the presence of traditional sex-role attitudes. Opposition to abortion is the product of a number of factors (especially religiosity). The findings in this chapter match more closely those of Granberg and others, rather than emphasizing the overarching importance of motherhood-sex-role attitudes, as in the Luker study.

The final major observation is the attitudinal similarity between activists and identifiers, as in the parallel efficacy scores, contrasted with the absence of activist behavior by the identifiers. This leaves us with a remarkable phenomenon—a group of non-activists who share activist orientations and concerns (though admittedly not usually in the same degree). When we add this to the absence of strong prior party/electoral attachments, we can reasonably conclude that this group represents a clear case of grassroots activation, as previously argued. Every other similar American study that comes to mind examines New Right/single-issue groups made up of individuals with some kind of prior activist background or orientation. Indeed, such groups are usually defined by their political activism. This cannot be said of the RTLP identifiers. These individuals do not even have the benefits of high levels of education or income. Yet they show an interest and motivation that is simply not customarily found among American non-activist voters. This observation provides an empirical case of the potency of abortion as a mobilizing issue. It also shows how a party system can respond when its structure makes some allowance for parties other than the two major ones.

NOTES

1. Daniel Callahan, *Abortion: Law, Choice and Morality* (New York: Macmillan, 1970); Jules Saltman and Stanley Zimmering, *Abortion Today* (Springfield, IL: Thomas, 1973); Patricia Steinhoff and Milton Diamond, *Abortion Politics* (Honolulu: University Press of Hawaii, 1977); James C. Mohr, *Abortion in America* (New York: Oxford University Press, 1978); Carl E. Schneider and Maris A. Vinovskis, eds., *The Law and Politics of Abortion* (Lexington, MA: Lexington Books, 1980); Frederick Jaffe et al., *Abortion Politics* (New York: McGraw-Hill, 1981); Raymond Tatalovich and Byron Daynes, *The Politics of Abortion* (New York: Praeger, 1981); Eva R. Rubin, *Abortion, Politics, and the Courts* (Westport, CT: Greenwood Press, 1982); Marilyn Falik, *Ideology and Abortion Policy Politics* (New York: Praeger, 1983); Gilbert Y. Steiner, ed., *The Abortion Dispute and the American System* (Washington, DC: Brookings Institution, 1983); Kristin Luker, *Abortion and the Politics of Motherhood* (Berkeley, CA: University of California Press, 1984).

2. Linda Bird Franke, *The Ambivalence of Abortion* (New York: Random House, 1978); John Noonan, *A Private Choice: Abortion in America in the Seventies* (New York: Free Press, 1979); Andrew H. Merton, *Enemies of Choice* (Boston: Beacon Press, 1981); Connie Paige, *The Right to Lifers* (New York: Summit Books, 1983).

3. See E. Patricia McCormick, *Attitudes Toward Abortion* (Lexington, MA: Lexington Books, 1975); Judith Blake, "Abortion and Public Opinion: The 1960–1970 Decade" *Science* 71 (February, 1971), 540–49; Donald Granberg, "Pro-Life or Reflection of Conservative Ideology?" An Analysis of Opposition to Legalized Abortion," *Sociology and Social Research* 62 (Winter, 1977/78), 414–29; B. Krishna Singh and Peter J. Leahy, "Contextual and Ideological Dimensions of Attitudes Toward Discretionary Abortion," *Demography* 15, 3 (1978), 381–88; Lucky M. Tedrow and E. R. Mahoney, "Trends in Attitudes Toward Abortion," *Public Opinion Quarterly* 43 (Summer, 1979), 181–89; Gallup Report, "Attitudes Toward Abortion Have Changed Little Since Mid–70s," *Gallup Report*, June, 1980, pp. 6–7; Pam Conover, Steve Coombs, and Virginia Gray, "The Attitudinal Roots of Single-Issue Politics," a paper presented at the 1980 Annual Meeting of the American Political Science Association, the Washington Hilton Hotel, Washington, DC, August 28–31; Judith Blake and Jorge H. Del Pinal, "Predicting Polar Attitudes Toward Abortion in the United States," in *Abortion Parley*, ed. James T. Burtchaell (Kansas

City, KA: Andrews and McMeel, Inc., 1980), pp. 29–56; Schneider and
Vinovskis, eds., *The Law and Politics of Abortion*, Ch. 6; Judith Blake and
Jorge H. Del Pinal, "Negativism, Equivocation, and Wobbly Assent,"
Demography 18, 3 (1981), 309–20; Jaffe et al., *Abortion Politics*, Ch. 8;
Sharon N. Barnartt and Richard J. Harris, "Recent Changes in Predictors
of Abortion Attitudes," *Sociology and Social Research* 66 (1982), 320–34.

4. Steinhoff and Diamond, *Abortion Politics*; Michael Margolis and
Kevin Neary, "Pressure Politics Revisited," *Policy Studies Journal*
(Spring, 1980), pp. 698–716; Donald Granberg, "The Abortion Activ-
ists," *Family Planning Perspectives* 13, 4 (July/August, 1981), 157–63; Joyce
Gelb and Marian Lief Palley, *Women and Public Policies* (Princeton, NJ:
Princeton University Press, 1982); Pamela Johnston Conover and Vir-
ginia Gray, *Feminism and the New Right* (New York: Praeger, 1983); Falik,
Ideology and Abortion Policy Politics; Pamela Johnston Conover, "The
Mobilization of the New Right," *Western Political Quarterly* (December,
1983), pp. 632–49; Luker, *Abortion and the Politics of Motherhood*, Chs. 5–
8.

5. David W. Brady and Kent L. Tedin, "Ladies in Pink: Religion
and Political Ideology in the Anti-ERA Movement, " *Social Science Quarterly* (March, 1976), p. 574.

6. Conover and Gray, *Feminism and the New Right*, pp. 103–5.

7. Ibid., pp. 107–11.

8. Granberg, "The Abortion Activists," pp. 158–61.

9. Granberg, "Pro-Life or Reflection of Conservative Ideology?"
pp. 417–24.

10. Luker, *Abortion and the Politics of Motherhood*, p. 197. Note similarities to the description of RTLP leader Ellen McCormack in Chapter
2.

11. Herbert McCloskey, Paul J. Hoffman, and Rosemary O'Hara,
"Issue Conflict and Consensus Among Party Leaders and Followers,"
American Political Science Review 54 (June, 1960), 406–27; Lester Milbrath,
Political Participation (Chicago: Rand McNally, 1965); Norman Luttbeg,
"The Structure of Beliefs Among Leaders and the Public," *Public Opinion
Quarterly* 32 (Fall, 1968), 398–409; Sidney Verba and Norman Nie, *Par-
ticipation in America* (New York: Harper and Row, 1972); John W. Ell-
wood and Robert J. Spitzer, "The Democratic National Telethons,"
Journal of Politics 41 (August, 1979), 828–64.

12. Party leaders declined to cooperate in providing a list of names
of party identifiers, and since no statewide voter enrollment lists are
kept by the State Board of Elections, I selected counties from around
the state, then selected names randomly from within these counties.
The upstate counties selected were Allegany, Cortland, Oneida, Seneca,

and Tompkins. Downstate counties included Bronx, Nassau, and Suffolk. This yielded a proportion in the sample of 105 upstate and 125 downstate respondents (this information was not available for an additional 19 respondents). The sample of state leaders was scattered widely around the state, but the upstate-downstate split among sampled leaders was about the same. This attempt to obtain information about voters from respective counties dramatized the wide array of recordkeeping practices in New York's counties. Some County Boards of Election were open and receptive. Some were hostile and uncommunicative. Some charged a nominal (or no) fee for obtaining lists of voters; others set fees in the hundreds of dollars. It is unfortunate that this public information is not made more uniformly and readily accessible to the public.

When possible, survey question wording was taken from Center for Political Study (CPS) University of Michigan surveys. Appendix 1 reproduces the questionnaire, and Appendix 2 lists 1984 RTLP enrollment for each of the state's 62 counties.

13. A study by Elms was based on a sample of 40; Brady and Tedin, 154; Conover and Gray, 107; Falik, 50 (both pro- *and* anti-); and Luker, 212 (also both pro- and anti-). Alan C. Elms, "Psychological Factors in Right-Wing Extremism," in *The American Right Wing*, ed. Robert A. Schoenberger (New York: Holt, Rinehart and Winston, 1969); Brady and Tedin, "Ladies in Pink"; Conover and Gray, *Feminism and the New Right*; Falik, *Ideology and Abortion Policy Politics*; Luker, *Abortion and the Politics of Motherhood*.

14. See Granberg, "The Abortion Activists," p. 159.

15. Luker, *Abortion and the Politics of Motherhood*, p. 194.

16. Granberg, "Pro-Life or Reflection of Conservative Ideology?" pp. 417–24.

17. Most agree that the Catholic church has been heavily involved in abortion politics, though there is relatively little literature on the subject. See Roger Williams, "The Power of Fetal Politics," *Saturday Review*, June 9, 1979, pp. 12–15; Jaffe et al., *Abortion Politics*, Ch. 6. By contrast, much has been written on the influence of the new Christian Right. See for example Michael Johnston, "The 'New Christian Right' in American Politics," *The Political Quarterly* 53, 2 (April-June, 1982), 181–99; Michael Lienesch, "Right-Wing Religion: Christian Conservatism as a Political Movement," *Political Science Quarterly* 97, 3 (Fall, 1982), 403–25; Carol Mueller, "In Search of a Constituency for the 'New Religious Right,' " *Public Opinion Quarterly* 47 (Summer, 1983), 213–29; Robert C. Liebman and Robert Wuthnow, eds., *The New Christian Right* (Hawthorne, New York: Aldine Publishing, 1983); Conover, "The Mo-

bilization of the New Right"; Arthur H. Miller and Martin P. Wattenberg, "Politics from the Pulpit: Religiosity and the 1980 Elections," *Public Opinion Quarterly* 48 (Spring, 1984), 301–17; and Kathleen M. Beatty and Oliver Walter, "Religious Preference and Practice: Reevaluating Their Impact on Political Tolerance," *Public Opinion Quarterly* 48 (Spring, 1984), 318–29.

I uncovered no systematic, verifiable, institutional link between the Catholic church and the RTLP; however, one party activist told me that a Catholic clergyman in Rockville Center, NY is a regular (and apparently influential) advisor to the top party leaders.

18. Conover and Gray, *Feminism and the New Right*, p. 49.

19. Brady and Tedin, "Ladies in Pink," p. 573.

20. Despite sharing an apparently closer ideological affinity with upstaters, the Conservative Party was formed with strong downstate influence. There is no evidence to indicate that the RTLP has pulled voters, resources, or personnel from the Conservative Party. This fact itself helps to confirm the observation that the RTLP has established a political base drawn mostly from the formerly uninvolved.

21. Luker, *Abortion and the Politics of Motherhood*, p. 193.

22. Ibid. See also Gelb and Palley, *Women and Public Policies*, Ch. 6.

4

PARTY DECAY, PARTY RENEWAL, AND HYBRID MULTI-PARTYISM

One of the premises of this volume has been the uniqueness of the New York multi-party system, in apparent contradistinction to America's two-party heritage. Yet it would be a mistake, I argue, to dismiss this case as a mere quirk pertinent only to state politics enthusiasts. The primary purpose of this final chapter will be to explore, in an admittedly polemical fashion, some of the consequences of the New York system for national party politics, by way of making a modest proposal for party change. Political analysts usually avoid explicit political prescriptions, in part at least because proposals are far easier to shoot down than to construct. But prescriptions can serve a number of intellectual purposes. They can serve to focus debate. They can provide a basis for subsequent reform, even if the end product is different from the initial proposal, and they also force the author to put him/herself "on the line," so to speak, by specifying (and thus clarifying) a general proposal. In any case, they enliven debate.

The other principal concern of this work, itself a consequence both of the New York system and social discontent about abortion practices, is of course the Right to Life Party. Regardless of how one feels about abortion, most would be quick to point to the RTLP as a case which demonstrates the baneful effects of even this kind of modified multi-party system. After all, the RTLP is a small party with a small constituency that has nevertheless exerted at least some, if marginal, influence; it is a party led by zealots disinclined to seek either compromise or the political center; it is a single issue party in a multi-issue world; and it raises an issue that most mainstream politicians would rather avoid.

Thus, the RTLP poses not only an intractable case, but perhaps the most difficult case imaginable for advocates of a party system that extends beyond the two major parties. At the same time, if the system can tolerate the most extreme case, it is tested sternly, and arguments in its favor are vastly strengthened. The RTLP provides just such a stern test.

As the previous examination of the RTLP shows, its actual influence has been small, and on the decline, precisely because of its single-issue, no-compromise zealotry. As example after example showed, these traits have had the effect of alienating both potential mainstream supporters and other elements of the right-to-life movement. So the very traits that would cause the greatest worry among two-party enthusiasts are precisely those that limit the RTLP's ability to exert greater influence.

The final observation about the RTLP—that it raises an issue that most in the major parties would rather avoid—speaks to a different question. Few would dispute the assertion that the major parties are sluggish to respond to new issues, schisms, and problems in society; yet, parties are performing an essential democratic function by doing so, and are avoiding this important function when they sidestep important issues. Thus, the RTLP is performing an important service if it helps compel the major parties to address a new, salient issue. But more will be said of this later. Before extrapolating from the New York case, a cursory assessment of parties today is in order.

THE STATE OF THE PARTIES

Evaluations of the current American party system are both varying and abundant. The most frequent assessment argues that American parties are in decline.[1] The synonyms frequently employed dramatize this dire conclusion: decay, disarray, atrophy, disintegration, decomposition, dealignment. Indeed, the rhetorical reverberations of some of these evaluations might be equally appropriate to describe the aftermath of a nuclear exchange. Nevertheless, the evidence marshalled to support the decline-of-parties thesis is extensive and impressive. Whether causes or symptoms of malaise, factors such as declining voter turnout, rising voter independence, increased voter suspicion of and alienation from parties and politics, declining party discipline and coherence within party hierarchies and among members of government (especially in legislative bodies), and greater competition from the media, interest groups, PACs and the like, all combine to produce a persuasive argument that parties are in deep trouble. And these are factors which affect all elements of parties—voters, leadership and organization, and those in government. As one political scientist observed, "In a world in which political scientists disagree on almost everything, there is remarkable agreement among the political science profession that the strength of American political parties has declined significantly over the past several decades. Regardless of how one measures partisanship—by personal party identification within the electorate, by party discipline in Congress, or by the vitality of party machinery—there is massive evidence attesting to the weakened condition of the parties in the United States."[2]

On the other hand, there are those who dispute the decline-of-parties thesis by arguing that parties are not so much declining as undergoing a process of transformation or adaptation.[3] Those subscribing to this view argue generally that the decline of parties has been overstated; that some of the indicators cited to prove the decline thesis have been misinterpreted; that in fact, in many ways, parties are organizationally stronger and more centralized than ever.[4]

Despite these variances in interpretation, one theme spans all of these arguments—namely, that the current party system is in need of renewal. In fact, the perceived need to strengthen the parties seems virtually unanimous among those who study party politics.[5] Thus, one need not believe that the parties are on the verge of extinction to support and promote measures to enhance their role. Given this pervasive sense that party renewal and reinvigoration is both necessary and desirable, and given too the enormous array of reforms and reform proposals that have been imposed on the parties over the years, I argue here that one central bias has inhibited attempts to enhance the role of parties. That bias has been America's persistent embrace of the two-party system as the ideal type. By clinging stubbornly to the principle of two-partyism (institutionally, intellectually, and emotionally), we ignore some important lessons of past party history, as well as those of an operational, if embryonic model of a hybrid multi-party system already adapted to the peculiarities of American party politics—i.e., the New York system.

THE LESSONS OF PARTY HISTORY

Party history has been clearly defined, with some minor disagreements, into five distinct partisan eras, each with its own policy agenda and political configuration.[6] The Massachusetts-and-Virginia-dominated Democratic-Republicans yielded to Jacksonian Democrats in the 1820s; Whigs yielded to the new Republican Party in the 1850s; new coalitions transformed the Republicans and Democrats in the 1890s, resulting in an era of Republican dominance; and the new Democratic Party of the 1930s brought together a coalition as alien to former Democratic standard-bearers like James Cox, Oscar W. Underwood, John W. Davis, and Al Smith as it was to the Republicans it derailed. In short, American party history is virtually defined by eras in which the existing political and policy agenda was displaced by new coalitions and new agendas. In each period, times of normalcy were disrupted by periods of instability, when dissidents realized that existing parties were no longer able, or inclined, to respond to new demands. Our generation has felt many of these kinds of rumblings, especially in the late 1960s and early 1970s. But the difference between this era and previous "critical" periods is the failure of existing parties to realign themselves in the manner of those in prior eras. Those periods take on particular importance precisely because parties were aligning themselves more closely to salient issues and concerns of the day. In addition, those periods were marked by enhanced political activity among voters and activists, greater attention to important contemporary issues and a generalized reinvigoration of politics.[7] Thus, the realignment process resembles, as much as anything, automobile tune-ups and alignments. In the absence of periodic adjustments, a car's performance efficiency will gradually and inexorably decline. Adjustments may be made gradually over a long period of time (comparable to V.O. Key's notion of political "secular realignment" occurring over a generation[8]), or all at once (a "critical realignment"[9]). Similarly, the "efficiency" (i.e., responsiveness, vitality, vigor) of a party system suffers in the absence of some kind of periodic adjustment or alignment. A key source responsible for the infusion of new ideas, interest, and zeal during realigning periods is third parties.

THE VITAL ROLE OF THIRD PARTIES

It is clear that the presence of active minor parties on the national level is affiliated with most of the important major political changes that have occurred in American politics. In his study of three realignment periods, Sundquist observed that for two of these periods, third parties were "the crux of the realignment story."[10] For the third period (the 1930s realignment), change occurred so quickly that full-blown third parties did not have a chance to materialize. But, as Sundquist concluded, "The threat of third-party activity, however, was a factor in keeping the New Deal on its activist course. . . ."[11]

Despite institutional bias, small size, and frequently short life span, third parties have played a vital role in the party process whenever they have appeared—though the relatively sparse literature on the general subject would seem to belie this fact.[12] Third parties are widely recognized as serving a number of important functions. They raise and dramatize new issues which often eventually lead to policy innovation, especially if minor-party proposals are later adopted by one of the major parties. Third parties serve as an electoral outlet by providing access to the electoral arena otherwise denied by the major parties. They also increase interest in politics, and serve an educative function by providing new information. And finally, they provide voters with alternative choices in the voting booth. Indeed, a recent study concluded that the level of third-party support among voters is directly related to dissatisfaction with the major parties.[13]

Third parties are of course subject to criticism as well. Criticisms generally fall into two categories: first, that minor parties threaten the stability of the political system by encouraging the splintering of electoral and governing coalitions; and second, that minor parties can thwart majority rule by depriving an otherwise likely winner of necessary support. These criticisms raise important questions that will be dealt with in a subsequent section.

Shortcomings notwithstanding, third parties play a vital but inadequately appreciated role in the party process—as is particularly evident during realignment periods. Especially pertinent to this role is serving as a watchdog of sorts on the major parties. As one observer noted, minor parties cast "penetrating light on the inner torments of the major part[ies]."[14] Another study concluded that third parties "are vehicles for aggregating and promoting citizen preferences. . . . Minor parties are not so much safety valves for voters who want to blow off steam as they are checks on the major parties. They are a weapon citizens can use to force the major parties to be more accountable . . . [and] are in fact necessary voices for the preservation of democracy."[15] From this assessment of third parties, it is indeed a small conceptual step to argue for an institutionalized inclusion of minor parties in the party system, by way of promoting the goal of party renewal (assuming that the potential problems posed by third parties can be dealt with satisfactorily). But before advancing to such a proposition, one other roadblock merits careful consideration—namely, two-partyism in American.

THE FOUNDATIONS OF TWO-PARTYISM

The historic explanations for America's persistent two-partyism are familiar enough. They include, first and foremost, a strong institutional bias, which incorporates single-member, plurality, winner-take-all electoral systems, a single nationally elected executive, election law regulations, the electoral college, the direct primary, and the like.[16] In addition, "social conditions" have played an important role. Americans are characterized as a pragmatic and relatively non-ideological people, allowing for the union of diverse coalitions under the two parties. Dualism seems to underlie most major historic issues (federalist vs. antifederalist, North vs. South, urban vs. rural, etc.), thus discouraging multi-factional splits and encouraging two-party opposition.[17] If the relative importance of these factors is debated, their cumulative consequence is not.

Yet the persistence of two-partyism in contemporary politics does not rest with these factors alone. Though these factors help to explain past trends, they hardly constitute an ironclad lid on other than two-party development. History is obviously replete with contradictions to pure two-partyism. There is, I argue, another dynamic at work—one evidenced in the absence of the realignment expected in the 1960s and 70s, and also in the persistence of a two-party "mythology."

HANGING ON FOR DEAR LIFE

I suggest that the two major parties have become so good at maintaining their hold on the electoral process that they have succeeded in short-circuiting the normal mechanisms that would otherwise yield a new party configuration, which itself helps to account for the stunted party politics of the last decade. This argument parallels similar assertions made about the Congress and the "vanishing marginals;"[18] namely, that congressmen have become so good at getting reelected that they have managed to insulate themselves from the normal political tides that would otherwise result in political alternation, despite mass disaffection with Congress as a whole. Clearly, two-party bias is not new to the last few decades. But the absence of a conventional realignment sequence has, de facto, left the remnants of the post–New Deal parties in control (though the dominant coalitions within the parties have been changing).[19] The existing bias, then, is in favor not only of two parties, but of the existing two parties—not necessarily out of any great love for them per se, but more out of anxiety for what might succeed them.

If these factors are widely discussed and acknowledged, one other factor is not: namely, the "mythology" surrounding two-partyism.[20] Despite widespread feelings that the two major parties are all but incapable of performing effectively in the current system, longstanding party myths promote a dogged kind of loyalty to two-partyism. To be fair, many factors beyond the control of the parties account for their inability to serve more effectively as mediating institutions. Nevertheless, the considerable difficulty the parties have had in adapting is rooted at least partly in our longstanding reverence for the two-party system.

THE FALSE IDOL—TWO-PARTY POLITICS

The American Political Science Association Committee on Political Parties provided in 1950 the classic statement about two-party politics—though the words could have been written as easily in 1900 or 1980: "The two-party system is so strongly rooted in the political traditions of this country and public preference for it is so well established that consideration of other possibilities seems entirely academic."[21] This statement contains a two-part argument. It says that the idea of a two-party system ought not to be questioned because: a) we have always had one, and b) the people like it. Even if we accept the first assertion as true, it is relatively unimportant. The fact of mere existence is no argument for continuance. This first assertion also implies that we should keep the two-party system because it has worked in the past. Without debating the merits of this supposition, it is clear that the widespread call for party renewal itself sweeps aside complacent acceptance of current party politics.

The second assertion—that the people are satisfied with the parties and the party system—is manifestly untrue. While there is some dispute as to whether popular views of the parties reflect marked antipathy[22] or rather a generalized feeling that parties are an irrelevancy,[23] it is abundantly clear that, at least in the eyes of most citizens, "parties just no longer matter much in the government process."[24] All that remains of "public preference" is the vestige of the two-party mythology.

THE PERVASIVENESS OF THE TWO-PARTY MYTH

The arguments propounding the virtues of a two-party system are imbedded deeply in the literature on parties. But the specific arguments made reveal more than a simple commitment to two parties.

To begin with, let us consider the generic strong points of a two-party system. In other words, what does a two-party (as distinct from a multi-party) system do best? It builds consensus, by offering two great umbrellas, each encompassing diverse factions. Factional differences are diffused, compromised, merged for the sake of governing. The virtue in this system is that it avoids anarchy in the electoral realm and paralysis in government (considered especially important in a large, heterogeneous nation). The obvious drawback is that it invariably suppresses legitimate viewpoints and concerns. Building majority coalitions is an instrumental component of this process. But the problem engendered by a two-alternative system is that a numerical majority may not represent a substantive majority. That is, if voters are given only two choices, one party will automatically receive majority support, regardless of substantive issue positions, the closeness of parties to voters, and the like. Thus, the two-party system itself fosters an image of satisfaction that may have little, if any, foundation. This was identified by William Riker as the problem of "artificial majorities."[25]

This overarching emphasis on consensus building and stability has a long history in the thoughtful consideration of American parties. Writing at the turn of the century, A. Lawrence Lowell, for example, emphasized the virtues of the consensus-building, opinion-aggregating function of parties, despite the attendant costs.

If political parties always distort public opinion in some degree, they also prevent still larger distortion caused by sudden waves of excitement. As great ecclesiastical bodies tend to frown upon religious excesses, so party organizations are inclined to check political vagaries. *They are essentially conservative, setting their faces against new experiments* [emphasis added].[26]

The need for mechanisms to build stable, workable coalitions is obvious—one need hardly invoke the cases of Weimar Germany or the French Fourth Republic. But what of the other extreme? What about a party system that works too well at building consensus? Here is a concern that has gone virtually unarticulated. Consider a more recent example—the case of a report published in 1982, authored by a group of distinguished party analysts, businessmen, and practitioners, brought together by the American Assembly to examine and prescribe remedies for the current party malaise. Quoting from the report, the guiding principle of their efforts was to fathom "how to reinforce the strength of political parties in order to improve *coherence of governance* [emphasis added]."[27] Voters have turned away from parties for many reasons; but I suggest that lack of "coherence" is not one. If anything, American parties suffer from too much coherence. It is the kind of coherence that make hamburg out of fillet, or baby food out of fresh fruit. Absent from this quote, and from the report as a whole, is a sustained concern for rebuilding the bridges between parties and people. Instead, much criticism and blame is heaped on what is viewed as the failed attempt to strengthen these links; that is, the party reforms of the 1960s and 1970s.[28]

I have no intention of defending recent party reforms. Rather, what is striking about the swelling number of party reform critics is the alternative they usually pose. Proposals invariably involve some version of a return to greater control by party regulars (most people would probably call them party "bosses"). The growing legitimacy of this anti-reform sentiment is abundantly evident within the Democratic Party, where for the first time in many years, the percentage of national delegates attending the 1984 presidential nominating convention who had been selected by party leaders and caucuses increased. Concomitantly, the number of primaries was down. In the Democratic party, 38 states held primaries in 1980; in 1984, the number was 25. In 1980, 72 percent of Democratic delegates were selected by primary. In 1984, the proportion was 54 percent, the lowest percent since 1968. This anti-reform reform movement is likely to satisfy party leaders but is equally sure to have no appreciable effect on voters' feelings about the overall state of the parties.

The anti-reformers in fact argue that the reforms have caused, or at least dramatically accelerated, party decay.[29] But this argument falters on two grounds. First, the downward cycle of party decomposition predates the implementation of reforms, which began with the relatively recent implementation of the McGovern-Fraser Commission recommendations in 1972—

though this is not to argue that the reforms have not had some adverse consequences. Second, it does not address the lingering conceptual flaw in the two-party model—namely, that the two-party system maximizes consensus building at the expense of the articulation of new, diverse, and salient points of view.[30] Whether the parties rely on a caucus or a primary system for nomination, voters are still left with a party mechanism that has shown itself to be structurally enfeebled, yet ever more firmly entrenched.

THE TWO PARTIES HOLD ALL THE CARDS, BUT HAVE NO CHIPS ...

The two major parties have succeeded almost completely in monopolizing the electoral process. Indeed, are there greater masters of consensus building among bi-party or multi-party systems in the world? I think not. Consider the data presented in Tables 4.1 and 4.2, and Figure 4.1. They illustrate the extent to which third parties have been locked out of governing since the advent of the New Deal (after the relatively furious third-party activity of the prior 40 years). The graph of third-party percentage of presidential vote illustrates the persistence of minor-party electoral efforts, despite a stacked political deck. Tables 4.1 and 4.2 demonstrate the failure of these efforts, as seen in the thousands of state executive and legislative races held each year.

My conclusion to this point is five-fold: 1) Legitimate third-party efforts continue, with more than a little support in the populace. (Consider the case on the presidential level of John Anderson. Though he received only 7 percent of the popular presidential vote in 1980, support for Anderson increased nine percent when pollsters asked voters their assessment of him if he had a real chance of winning. At one point, his standing in the polls was almost 25 percent.)[31] 2) The major parties will not willingly relinquish control of their own structures. 3) The major parties cannot be forced from within to significantly enhance their responsiveness in a way that would reinvigorate popular support and loyalty. That, indeed, is the lesson of recent party reform. 4) If we cannot rely on new coalitions within the old

Table 4.1
Elected State Executive Officials for the 50 States

Year	Total elective officials	Number belonging to minor party	Percent
1979	301	0	0%
1977	303	6	1.9
1975	302	0	0
1973	306	1	0.3
1971	298	3	1.0
1969	189	1	0.5
1967	189	1	0.5

Source: Council of State Governments, State Elective Officials and the Legislatures.

parties, then we should consider some new parties (Schattsch-neider seemed to anticipate the failures of party reform when he said, "Democracy is not to be found *in* the parties but *between* the parties.")[32] 5) Most of the electoral establishment would cer-tainly recoil at the prospect of a new, untried party configura-tion—especially one alien to American experience. Enter New York's multi-party system.

THE CASE OF NEW YORK

New York politics have been and continue to be dominated by the two major parties. Yet, discussion in previous chapters demonstrates the importance of New York's minor parties. But before assessing the consequences of this multi-party system,

Table 4.2
State Legislators of the 50 States

Year	Total number of legislators	Number belonging to minor party	Percent
1983	7438	11	0.1%
1981	7482	11	0.1
1979	7482	11	0.1
1977	7562	14	0.2
1975	7565	27	0.4
1973	7563	26	0.3
1971	7750	17	0.2
1969	7731	5	0.06
1967	7665	5	0.07
1965	7937	9	0.1
1963	7913	63	0.8
1961	7900	7	0.09
1959	7879	8	0.1
1957	7827	22	0.3
1955	7778	53	0.7
1953	7749	51	0.7
1951	7675	57	0.7
1949	7636	80	1.0
1947	7633	28	0.4
1945	7455	20	0.3
1942	7500	43	0.6
1940	7495	34	0.5
1938	7481	68	0.9

Source: The Council of State Governments, The Book of the States.

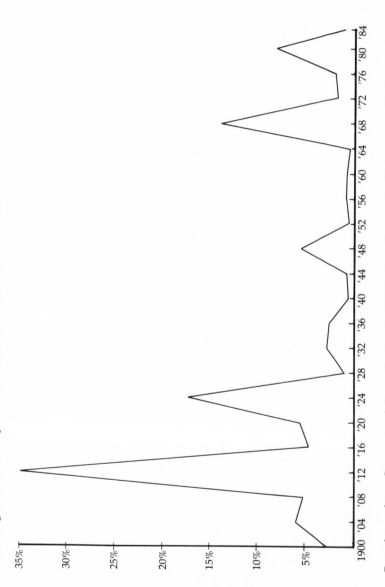

Figure 4.1
Percentage of Third-Party Vote in Presidential Elections, 1900–1984

Data drawn from: Congressional Quarterly, Presidential Elections Since 1789 (Washington D.C.: CQ Press, 1979)

let us clarify the question of whether, in fact, New York can be labeled multi-party.

Counting the parties

The U.S. is invariably classified as a two-party system, despite the presence of numerous other parties. In 1976, for example, eight other political parties fielded presidential candidates that appeared on the ballot in at least ten states. What, then, makes New York different?

Maurice Duverger argued in his classic work that the number of parties was the prime determinant of a party system.[33] Sartori refined that concept by setting out two criteria or conditions that resolve the question of whether a minor party can be considered significant in a political system. The first, coalition potential, involves the saliency of a party in forming a governing coalition. If a party is never needed to form a governing coalition, it cannot fulfill this criterion of party significance. The second criterion is blackmail potential. Does a party have the ability to extract concessions from others in the electoral arena, in exchange for its support? If either of these conditions holds, a party can be considered significant, and should be counted.[34] The first condition does not strictly apply in a non-parliamentary system, since coalitions are formed within parties before elections are held. Nevertheless, other research has demonstrated that the minor parties in New York do have an impact on policymaking in state government, especially in the state legislature, despite the fact that virtually no members of the legislature are elected on a minor-party line alone.[35] The second criterion, blackmail potential, is clearly demonstrated by the minor parties, evidenced in their successful use of the cross-endorsement rule to extract favors and concessions from the major parties (see Chapter 1). Thus, New York's minor parties pose no threat to supplant the major parties (leaving their hegemony intact), but neither can they be ignored by the major parties. The minor parties can endure precisely because they can do without the one thing other minor parties have always needed—that is, electing their own to office. And the minor parties pose no threat to two-partyism in governing. A minor party could one day gain electoral ascendency, but that need not occur for the party to continue to serve as an electoral outlet, and if it does, then it should be accepted as a legitimate expression of popular will.

PUSHING THE VIRTUES OF THE MULTI-PARTY SYSTEM TO THE LIMIT: THE CASE OF THE RTLP

Even critics of New York's multi-party system have come to tolerate the relatively orthodox Liberal and Conservative Parties, grumblings from major party leaders notwithstanding. But criticism has become more strident over the newest entrant, the RTLP. As mentioned, it differs from the other state parties in at least three aspects: 1) its single-issue orientation—that of an unswerving commitment to ending abortion; 2) its ideological rigidity and zeal; and 3) the unwillingness of its leaders to enter into traditional bargaining and compromising. The party leaders in fact pride themselves on their refusal to compromise on the issue.

Before discussing the ramifications of the RTLP case, let us first consider the overall multi-party model, but do so with the understanding that it offers a viable party model worthy of replication on the national level.[36] As I argued earlier, the major parties have become ever better at monopolizing party politics. In previous electoral eras, third parties were often vehicles for issues and concerns that could find no other electoral route. Parties that represented widely felt sentiments either grew, or were in some respect subsumed or co-opted by a major party. Thus it was that the rise of minor parties was invariably associated with important and necessary political changes in our history. In the current era, however, minor party concerns can be more easily ignored by the major parties, especially given the wide array of legal devices at the disposal of major parties. To further the suppression of minor parties, given historical patterns, is to further erode the health of the American party system.

One of the virtues of the New York model is that it preserves a certain degree of major-party hegemony. Given the nation's historic devotion to two-partyism the likelihood of national parties evolving into an Italian-like system, for example, is at best highly unlikely.

Criticisms of the New York system

A principal opponent of the New York multi-party system, Howard Scarrow, summarizes four arguments against the system. First, he argues that the state's minor parties wield influence beyond their actual degree of electoral support. Second, he says that the system has spawned cynicism and an obsession with patronage. Third, he argues that the cross-endorsement system, by allowing several parties to list the same candidate, actually narrows voter choices. And fourth, he decries the likelihood of a minority electoral outcome.[37]

To deal with each criticism in order, it is true that, in at least some circumstances, third parties in New York do exercise influence beyond their size, and examples have been provided in previous chapters. The irony of this reality lies in the fact that, as the RTLP case shows, this influence is often engendered by political insecurity rather than concrete clout. But beyond this, for such parties to indeed have any clout (with political leaders *and* voters) they must be able to cast a larger shadow—especially at the national level, since the deck is otherwise so heavily stacked in favor of the major parties. Nothing less will do.

Second, the concern that the New York system has spawned cynicism and an obsession with patronage seems to be a false concern. Clearly, the RTLP is utterly unconcerned with the latter. And even the Liberals and Conservatives have programmatic issue concerns that are evident and laudable, if one believes in promoting at least some issue consciousness in the political realm.[38] But also, what is noxious about an interest in patronage? It is certainly a mainstay of the major parties in New York, even in this day and age. Are the minor parties to be judged by higher standards of political conduct?

Scarrow's third assertion—that the number of candidates does not equal the number of parties—is certainly true, precisely because of cross-endorsement. Nevertheless, voters in New York still have more electoral choices because of the minor parties than they would otherwise. Moreover, the minor parties can actually help refine major-party choices. For example, a Democratic candidate who also holds the Conservative and RTLP endorsements transmits a far more precise message to voters about his/her ideological predilections. Thus, the added endorsements provided by the minor parties can enhance the number and precision of political cues available to voters, thereby facilitating voter choice.

Finally, minority electoral outcomes do sometimes, if rarely, occur. But this problem can easily be remedied by implementing a run-off provision, as is used in many big-city mayoral races. Or, perhaps a more satisfactory alternative is found in "approval voting."[39] This system of voting allows voters to register preferences for more than one candidate in a multi-candidate race, thereby helping to insure that the condorcet, or majority candidate (the one actually preferred by most voters, instead of the one with the largest plurality of vote), is in fact the one selected. This system has been widely discussed in the political science literature and has been proposed in the New York and Vermont legislatures.[40]

Fears persist in America that any significant nationwide move toward a multi-party system will inexorably lead the country into an ungovernable multi-party morass. But this fear ignores the fundamental reality that a party system is principally a reflection of the nation's society. In America, the two-party tradition will not go the way of the carrier pigeon, any more than it has in New York. Extreme examples like those of the French Fourth Republic and Weimar Germany cannot be disconnected from their respective political, social, and cultural milieus.

Some share the concern that multi-party systems are ultimately less democratic, less responsive, less stable, or more prone to violence than two-party systems. But detailed research contradicts this assumption, finding no measurable difference between two- and multi-party systems in terms of these factors.[41] Again, party systems do not exist in a vacuum, and the the New York system is not a transplant from another culture. It is a native American adaptation.

New York as a model

And what of New York? Though it is difficult to disentangle cause and consequence, it is true that New York has consistently been evaluated as having a competitive and vigorous party system, according to a 50–state ranking of party competitiveness spanning a period from 1956 to 1980.[42] New York also rates high in legislative party cohesion.[43] Another study concluded that "New York state and its subdivisions have the strongest parties in the nation."[44] So for what it is worth, the New York party system as a whole compares well with the systems of other states in terms of values considered important for measuring party vigor. Naturally, this does not prove that New York's minor parties have enhanced party strength, competitiveness, and the like. Nor can the minor parties be divorced from the state's competitive partisan tradition. But given everything we know about the functions of minor parties, the conclusion that the New York system enhances party vitality is almost inescapable. And the New York system itself demonstrates that multiple parties can exist without breaking down two-partyism.

And what of the RTLP case? Electorally, it has demonstrated a fairly consistent, though declining, average vote-getting level. Though the party can offer a fairly consistent vote to interested candidates, its actual influence has probably been exaggerated by the trepidations of insecure political candidates scrapping for votes. This reliance on reputational power is the key to its success, especially since the prospects for increasing its vote base are slim, given its single-issue tunnel vision. Indeed, this tunnel vision is both the characteristic that identifies it as a single-issue party, and the one that keeps it from posing a more serious challenge to the other parties. The RTLP cannot hope to establish the kind of bargaining position of the other minor parties in New York vis-à-vis the major parties, for the simple reason that elections in America seldom if ever revolve around single issues. The party's refusal to bargain on the abortion issue further diminishes its electoral flexibility. The RTLP offers a hypothetical model of action for other similar movements, but it is not one that shakes the foundation of the multi-party model. In fact, it is the example that illustrates the system's continued commitment to consensus building and overall moderation. The RTLP is probably on the wane—but not because it has achieved its goals, despite the commitment and zeal of its adherents. The New York system opens the door to zealotry; but this concern is not a new one in American politics. It was precisely the worry about the excesses of faction that caused James Madison to write *Federalist* #10. He concluded that the benefits of liberty and freedom outweighed the possible adverse consequences of faction. Similarly, the advantages of an American multi-party system can also stand the stresses of single-issueism and zealotry. Consensus building, compromise, and stability are too deeply ingrained in the American political psyche for any other pattern to obtain. And if a reinvigoration of parties is to take place, allowance must be made for electoral contentiousness. If it is not, then we can only expect an ever-accelerating slide away from meaningful, vital party politics. If we are to encourage meaningful party politics, we must also be prepared to accept the presence of causes that are, to some, odious.

NOTES

1. For example, David Broder, *The Party's Over* (New York: Harper and Row, 1971); Walter Dean Burnham, *Critical Elections* (New York: W. W. Norton, 1970); Philip E. Converse, "Change in the American Electorate," in *The Human Meaning of Social Change*, ed. Angus Campbell and Philip Converse (New York: Russell Sage Foundation, 1972); Norman Nie, Sidney Verba, and John R. Petrocik, *The Changing American Voter* (Cambridge: Harvard University Press, 1976); Everett C. Ladd, *Where Have All the Voters Gone?* (New York: W. W. Norton, 1977); William J. Crotty and Gary C. Jacobson, *American Parties in Decline* (Boston: Little, Brown, 1980); Martin P. Wattenberg, *The Decline of American Political Parties, 1952–1980* (Cambridge: Harvard University Press, 1984); Ruth K. Scott and Ronald J. Hrebenar, *Parties in Crisis* (New York: Wiley, 1984).

2. Gary R. Orren, "The Changing Styles of American Party Politics," in *The Future of American Political Parties*, ed. Joel L. Fleishman (Englewood Cliffs, NJ: Prentice-Hall, 1982), p. 31.

3. Alan Gitelson, M. Margaret Conway, and Frank B. Feigert, *American Political Parties: Stability and Change* (Boston: Houghton Mifflin, 1984); Joseph A. Schlesinger, "The New American Political Party," a paper presented at the 1984 Annual Meeting of the American Political Science Association, the Washington Hilton, Washington, DC, August 30–September 2; James L. Gibson et al., "Assessing Party Organizational Strength," *American Journal of Political Science* 27, 2 (May, 1983), 193–222; James L. Sundquist, "Whither the American Party System?— Revisited," *Political Science Quarterly* (Winter, 1983–84), pp. 573–93; Xan-

dra Kayden and Eddie Mahe, Jr., *The Party Goes On* (New York: Basic Books, 1985).

4. See in particular, Gitelson, Conway, and Feigert, *American Political Parties*.

5. Gerald M. Pomper, ed., *Party Renewal in America* (New York: Praeger, 1980); David E. Price, *Bringing Back the Parties* (Washington, DC: Congressional Quarterly Press, 1984); The American Assembly, Columbia University, "The Future of American Political Parties," The Sixty-second American Assembly, April 15–18, 1982, Arden House, Harriman, NY; President's Commission for a National Agenda for the Eighties, *The Electoral and Democratic Process in the Eighties*, Paul G. Rogers, Chairperson (Englewood Cliffs, NJ: Prentice-Hall, 1981). See also the work and publications of the Committee for Party Renewal. Their publication, *Party Line*, is published at the Eagleton Institute of Politics, Rutgers University. The organization includes a wide array of political scientists, political activists, and leaders. Their interests are both academic and pragmatic. As Leon D. Epstein observed, "The professional commitment of political scientists to the desirability of political parties has a substantial history." "The Scholarly Commitment to Parties," in *Political Science: The State of the Discipline*, ed. Ada W. Finifter (Washington, DC: American Political Science Association, 1983), p. 127.

6. Walter Dean Burnham, "The Changing Shape of the American Political Universe," *American Political Science Review* (March, 1965), pp. 3–27; James Sundquist, *Dynamics of the Party System* (Washington, DC: Brookings Institution, 1973); William N. Chambers and Walter Dean Burnham, eds., *The American Party System* (New York: Oxford University Press, 1975); Benjamin Ginsberg, "Elections and Public Policy," *American Political Science Review* (March, 1976), pp. 41–49; Paul Kleppner et al., *The Evolution of American Electoral Systems* (Westport, CT: Greenwood Press, 1981).

7. Sundquist, *Dynamics of the Party System*, Chs. 1–3.

8. V. O. Key, "Secular Realignment and the Party System," *Journal of Politics*, 21 (May, 1959), 198–210.

9. The distinction between "critical" and "secular" realignments is made in Burnham, *Critical Elections*, Ch. 1.

10. Sundquist, *Dynamics of the Party System* (1983 ed.), p. 313.

11. Ibid.

12. While there are many studies of particular third parties, there is relatively little on the general subject. Existing general works focus almost exclusively on presidentially-centered third-party efforts. See Fred E. Haynes, *Third Party Movements Since the Civil War* (Iowa City, IA: State Historical Society, 1916); William B. Hesseltine, *The Rise and*

Fall of Third Parties (Washington, DC: Public Affairs Press, 1948); Howard P. Nash, *Third Parties in American Politics* (Washington, DC: Public Affairs Press, 1959); William B. Hesseltine, *Third Party Movements in the United States* (New York: Van Nostrand, 1962); Murray S. Stedman and Susan Stedman, *Discontent at the Polls* (New York: Russell and Russell, 1967); Daniel A. Mazmanian, *Third Parties in Presidential Elections* (Washington, DC: Brookings Institution, 1974); Howard R. Penniman, "Presidential Third Parties and the Modern American Two-Party System," in *The Party Symbol*, ed. William Crotty (San Francisco: W. H. Freeman, 1980), pp. 101–18; Frank Smallwood, *The Other Candidates* (Hanover, NH: University Press of New England, 1983); Steven J. Rosenstone, Roy L. Behr, and Edward Lazarus, *Third Parties in America* (Princeton, NJ: Princeton University Press, 1984). Two useful reference works on third parties are Paul H. Blackman, *Third Party President?* (Washington, DC: Heritage Foundation, 1976); and D. Stephen Rockwood et al., *American Third Parties Since the Civil War* (New York: Garland Publishing, 1985).

13. Rosenstone, Behr, and Lazarus, *Third Parties in America*, pp. 215–16, 221–24. See also Hesseltine, *The Rise and Fall of Third Parties*, pp. 9–10; Austin Ranney and Willmoore Kendall, *Democracy and the American Party System* (New York: Harcourt, Brace, 1956), Chs. 18–19; Burnham, *Critical Elections*, Ch. 1; Mazmanian, *Third Parties in Presidential Elections*, Ch. 3; Smallwood, *The Other Candidates*, pp. 25–27.

14. Samuel Lubell, *The Future of American Politics*, (New York: Doubleday, 1956), p. 217.

15. Rosenstone, Behr, and Lazarus, *Third Parties in America*, p. 222.

16. There are many examples of how the major parties rely on institutional mechanisms to enforce two-partyism. To take a small example, consider campaign finance reform. The Federal Election Campaign Act (FECA) of 1974 provides major-party presidential candidates with matching funds at the start of the campaign. Minor parties, however, receive funding after the election, if they poll at least 5 percent of the vote. In addition, even if a third party does exceptionally well, the FECA guarantees equal funding for the Republicans and Democrats, whereas minor parties receive funding based on a formula that awards less money even if the third party does as well as a major party. Also, the major parties are given funds for holding nominating conventions, whereas minor parties are not. See Nelson Polsby, *Consequences of Party Reform* (New York: Oxford University Press, 1983), p. 83.

17. Gerald Pomper, *Elections in America* (New York: Dodd, Mead, 1968), pp. 46–50; Benjamin Ginsberg, *The Consequences of Consent* (Reading, MA: Addison-Wesley, 1982), pp. 145–52.

18. See David R. Mayhew, "Congressional Elections: The Case of the Vanishing Marginals," *Polity* 6 (1974), 298–302; Albert D. Cover and David R. Mayhew, "Congressional Dynamics and the Decline of Competitive Congressional Elections," in *Congress Reconsidered*, ed. Lawrence C. Dodd and Bruce I. Oppenheimer (Washington, DC: Congressional Quarterly Press, 1981), pp. 62–83; Morris Fiorina, *Congress: Keystone of the Washington Establishment* (New Haven, CT: Yale University Press, 1977).

19. See Benjamin Ginsberg and Martin Shefter, "A Critical Realignment? The New Politics, the Reconstituted Right, and the Election of 1984," in *The Elections of 1984*, ed. Michael Nelson (Washington, DC: Congressional Quarterly Press, 1985).

20. See Theodore J. Lowi, "Toward a More Responsible Three-Party System," *PS* (Fall, 1983), pp. 699–706.

21. Committee on Responsible Parties, American Political Science Association, *Toward a More Responsible Two-Party System* (New York: Rinehart and Co., 1950), p. 18. Clinton Rossiter was less diplomatic: " . . . we live under a persistent, obdurate, one might almost say *tyrannical*, two-party system." *Parties and Politics in America* (Ithaca, NY: Cornell University Press, 1960), p. 3.

22. Nie, Verba, and Petrocik, *The Changing American Voter*, pp. 57–58; Price, *Bringing Back the Parties*, pp,. 16–18; Smallwood, *The Other Candidates*, pp. 278–82.

23. Wattenberg, *The Decline of American Political Parties*, p. xv.

24. Ibid.

25. William Riker, *Democracy in the United States* (New York: Macmillan, 1953), pp. 108–9. See also, Theodore J. Lowi, *Incomplete Conquest* (New York: Holt, Rinehart and Winston, 1981), p. 225.

26. Quoted in Austin Ranney, *The Doctrine of Responsible Party Government* (Urbana, IL: University of Illinois Press, 1954), p. 56.

27. American Assembly, "The Future of American Political Parties," p. 2.

28. Ibid., pp. 7–11. See also Polsby, *Consequences of Party Reform*; Austin Ranney, *Curing the Mischiefs of Faction* (Berkeley, CA: University of California Press, 1975), Ch. 6; Ladd, *Where Have All the Voters Gone?*, Ch. 3; Jeane Kirkpatrick, *Dismantling the Parties* (Washington, DC: American Enterprise Institute, 1978).

29. For example, Kirkpatrick, *Dismantling the Parties*, p. 2; Polsby, *Consequences of Party Reform*, passim.

30. This argument is made in Ginsberg, *The Consequences of Consent*, pp. 152–58.

31. Rosenstone, Behr, and Lazarus, *Third Parties in America*, pp. 39–41.

32. E. E. Schattschneider, *Party Government* (New York: Holt, Rinehart and Winston, 1942), p. 60. V. O. Key makes the same point about parties in his writings.

33. Maurice Duverger, *Political Parties* (New York: Wiley, 1954), p. 206.

34. Giovanni Sartori, *Parties and Party Systems* (New York: Cambridge University Press, 1976), pp. 122–24.

35. Mazmanian, *Third Parties in Presidential Elections*, pp. 130, 132; Howard Scarrow, *Parties, Elections, and Representation in the State of New York* (New York: New York University Press, 1983), pp. 71–73. Scarrow examines this question closely for the state legislature, and argues that the link between legislative behavior and minor-party endorsement can occur in one of three ways: 1) major-party candidates can be recruited from the minor parties (this rarely happens); 2) the minor parties can press the major parties to nominate favored and sympathetic candidates, and withhold a minor party nod if the major party candidate is unacceptable (this tactic is effective); and 3) the minor parties may threaten to withhold an endorsement from a legislator who does not conform any longer to party principles (also an effective tactic). The methodological problem is that measuring this kind of influence is often difficult. Based on his evidence, however, Scarrow is able to conclude that "the minor parties have, on the whole, lived up to their proclaimed objective of backing legislators of the appropriate ideological leanings." (p. 70)

36. Daniel Mazmanian also finds virtue in the New York system. See *Third Parties in Presidential Elections*, pp. 134–35.

37. Scarrow, *Parties, Elections, and Representation*, pp. 73–75. Scarrow is careful to point out, however, that he is not opposed to multi-partyism per se, but he does not view New York's minor parties as true parties.

38. The programmatic, issue concerns of the Liberals and Conservatives are discussed in Mazmanian, *Third Parties in Presidential Elections*, pp. 130–32.

39. See Steven J. Brams and Peter Fishburn, *Approval Voting* (Boston: Birkhauser, 1983).

40. Some recent articles include Richard G. Niemi, "The Problem of Strategic Behavior Under Approval Voting," *American Political Science Review* 78, 4 (December, 1984), 952–58; Gary W. Cox, "Strategic Electoral Choice in Multi-Member Districts: Approval Voting in Practice?" *American Journal of Political Science* 28, 4 (November, 1984), 722–38; Theodore S. Arrington and Saul Brenner, "Another Look at Approval Voting," *Polity* 17, 1 (Fall, 1984), 118–34, 144; Steven J. Brams and Peter C. Fishburn, "A Careful Look at 'Another Look at Approval Voting.' "

Polity 17, 1 (Fall, 1984), 135–43. Both proponents and opponents of approval voting seem to agree that the system would not give any special advantage to non-centrist candidates. See last two articles.

41. G. Bingham Powell, "Party Systems and Political System Performance," *American Political Science Review* (December, 1981), pp. 861–79. See also Lawrence Dodd, *Coalitions in Parliamentary Governments* (Princeton, NJ: Princeton University Press, 1976). Sartori concludes that the best predictor of system stability, in comparing types of party systems, is the number and strength of anti-system parties (those parties that do not accept the legitimacy of the regime). *Parties and Party Systems*, p. 318.

42. Austin Ranney, "Parties in State Politics," in *Politics in the American States*, ed. Herbert Jacob and Kenneth Vines, 2nd ed.; and John F. Bibby et al., "Parties in State Politics," in *Politics in the American States*, ed. Virginia Gray, Herbert Jacob, and Kenneth Vines, 4th ed., (Boston: Little, Brown, 1971, 1983), p. 66, p. 87, respectively. Also, see Samuel C. Patterson and Gregory A. Caldeira, "The Etiology of Partisan Competition," *American Political Science Review* 78, 3 (September, 1984), 691–707. Aside from confirming the results of other studies—that New York has a vigorous and competitive party system—the authors conclude that the organizational strength of the parties in a state is a major determinant of vigorous party competition. This explanation emphasizes the conclusion that parties themselves can shape the quality of the electoral environment (as opposed to factors such as socioeconomic complexity and other politico-cultural factors which, while also having an impact on party competitiveness, cannot be manipulated by political structures). In other words, the nature and quality (and quantity) of parties can affirmatively influence the partisan environment, which is precisely the objective of the reform proposed in this chapter.

43. Ranney, "Parties in State Politics," p. 113.

44. Howard A. Scarrow, "The Strength of New York's Political Parties," a paper presented at the Annual Meeting of the New York State Political Science Association, Albany, NY, April 6–7, 1984, p. 13.

EPILOGUE

When politics and technology collide, it is usually to the detriment of both. History is littered with examples of each befouling the other, and of false claims made by each that it could solve the other's problems. Yet it is conceivable that advances in medical technology may, in a few years, largely defuse the abortion question. French scientists have developed a drug, called RU–486, that can prevent a fertilized egg from implanting in the uterus and, if implanted, can cause it to be sloughed off. The drug thus can have both contraceptive and abortive effect (and is appropriately labeled a "contragestive"). A woman taking this pill would consequently not face a prolonged pregnancy, but she might not ever know if this consequence was the result of contraceptive or abortive action by the drug. Such a difference might seem inconsequential, but a pill that could end an early pregnancy without the involvement of doctors or others would dramatically privatize abortion, as it would work up to the sixth week of pregnancy, and combine the up-to-now separate processes of contraception and abortion. It would also take much of the steam out of the anti-abortion movement that now promotes its perspective by dramatizing the human-like features of later-stage aborted fetuses (as in the 12–week-old fetus discussed in the anti-abortion film "The Silent Scream"), and by identifying and targeting both the women who seek abortions and the places that they are conducted.[1] RU–486 is still experimental as of this writing and, if proven safe and efficacious, will not be available for some years.

Even if the abortion debate ended tomorrow, however, it would be no less revealing as an example of an intractable political issue. We have seen, from Chapter 1, that abortion is not unique as a single issue inducing a wide range of political action, including the establishment of a political party devoted to a sole cause. Table 1.1 summarized ten characteristics of past single-issue parties. The subsequent examination of the Right to Life Party revealed its consonance with all of these traits. The RTLP exhibited a bi-factional split within its ranks between narrow purists and more pragmatic compromisers; it is part of a broader social movement raising an issue not clearly addressed by the major parties; the party is perceived as the most zealous element in the overall political movement (and certainly within the context of New York politics); it elevated issue purity above electoral success; it emphasized political education as a key goal; its origins were indisputably grassroots; it succeeded in introducing a salient issue; it has sought a constitutional remedy; the issue itself is highly emotive in nature, and has been framed in moral terms; and finally, religious leaders have played a key role in the movement and the party. The RTLP stands in close company, analytically, with past single-issue parties.

The comparison might be criticized by arguing that the RTLP is not a significant case, whether it shares similarities with past single-issue parties or not, because of its mostly single-state boundedness. The other parties examined all had national ambitions, and at one time or another, all had organizations in many states. The RTLP has national ambitions, too. What it lacks is a national electoral environment where such ambitions for a grassroots party can be more easily realized. Third parties that have received national attention in this century have coalesced around national figures, and are in that sense "top-down" parties. The grassroots or "bottom-up" party has had a far more difficult time in this century. Minor parties have needed the added draw of a known national leader to help overcome the web of rules, norms and biases that have made the electoral system even less hospitable to other parties. Despite the more limited reach of the RTLP, then, it is functionally equivalent to prior single-issue parties, and is therefore comparable.

A final word about values that are and are not expressed in

this book. No attempt has been made to judge the RTLP, or the competing interests enmeshed in the abortion dispute. A strong value has been promoted, however, about the electoral playing field upon which the abortion struggle has taken place. This value is that, in the partisan arena, all will benefit—including players and spectators—if more than two partisan teams are allowed to compete. Multi-party politics is no panacea; but given the current state of the parties, related electoral conditions, the underlying durability of the system, and the Americanized multi-party blueprint embodied by the case of New York State, such an option for America is both in keeping with our electoral traditions and principles, and indeed likely to be invigorating for an electoral system in need of invigoration. The likelihood of the adoption of such changes on a broad scale in the near future is, aside from being small, probably less significant than the conditions that impel their suggestion.

NOTES

1. See Ellen Goodman, "A New Twist in Abortion Debate," *Syracuse Post-Standard*, February 28, 1986.

APPENDIX 1

QUESTIONNAIRE

Please write the number of your answer on the lines at the left.

1). Before joining the Right to Life Party (RTLP), what was your prior party
enrollment? 1. Democrat 2. Republican 3. Conservative 4. Liberal 5. Inde-
_____ pendent 6. not enrolled; didn't vote 7. other_____.

2). Who did you vote for in the 1980 presidential election? 1. Ronald Reagan 2. Jim-
_____ my Carter 3. John Anderson 4. Ellen McCormack 5. other 6. didn't vote

3). Who did you vote for in the 1982 New York governor's race? 1. Mario Cuomo 2.
_____ Lew Lehrman 3. Robert Bohner 4. other 5. didn't vote

4). Have you ever worn campaign buttons, or put political (bumper) stickers on
_____ your car? 1. yes 2. no

5). Have you ever attended political meetings, rallies, dinners or things like
_____ that? 1. yes 2. no

6). Have you ever done any active work for a political candidate, group or party
_____ (such as canvassing, handing out leaflets, telephoning, etc.)? 1. yes 2. no

7). Have you ever contributed money to a political party, group or candidate?
_____ 1. yes 2. no

8). Do you follow government and public affairs in the news: 1. most of the time
_____ 2. some of the time 3. only now and then 4. hardly at all

9). Which do you prefer: 1. to vote for Right to Life Party (RTLP) candidates on
_____ the RTLP line, or 2. to vote for candidates running on the Republican or Democratic line that are also endorsed by the RTLP

10). Both the Republicans and Democrats have been criticized for not being sympathetic enough to right to life concerns. But which party seems closer to the
_____ right to life view: 1. Republicans 2. Democrats

11). Have you ever written a letter to the editor of a newspaper or public of-
_____ ficial about abortion? 1. yes 2. no

12). Have you ever engaged in activities to protest abortion, such as sign pe-
_____ titions, attend meetings, or things like that? 1. yes 2. no

_____ 13). Do you feel that abortions should: 1. never be allowed 2. be allowed only
when the life of the mother is at stake 3. be allowed in cases of rape or incest
(in addition to life of the mother at stake) 4. be allowed if the woman would
have difficulty caring for the child 5. be allowed or not according to the conscience and judgment of the woman 6. other_____.

14). Do you ever talk about the abortion issue with friends or others (for this
_____ question, indicate all appropriate answers at left): 1. at home 2. at work
3. at church 4. at social occasions 5. almost never 6. other_____.

_____ 15).Which of these statements do you agree with? 1. many qualified women can't
get good jobs; men with the same skills have much less trouble; or 2. in general,
men are more qualified than women for jobs that have great responsibility.

_____ 16). Which of these two statements do you agree with? 1. It's more natural for
men to have the top responsible jobs in the country; or 2. sex discrimination
keeps women from the top jobs.

_____ 17). Which of the following two statements do you agree with? 1. by nature women
are happiest when they are making a home and caring for children; or 2. our
society, not nature, teaches women to prefer homemaking to work outside the home.

_____ 18). People like me don't have any say about what the government does. Do you:
1. agree 2. disagree 3. no opinion

19). Voting is the only way people like me can have any say about how the govern-
_____ ment runs things. Do you: 1. agree 2. disagree 3. no opinion

20). Sometimes politics and government seem so complicated that a person like me
_____ can't really understand what's going on. Do you: 1. agree 2. disagree 3. no opinion

21). I don't think public officials care much what people like me think. Do
_____ you: 1. agree 2. disagree 3. no opinion

22). Do you think that people in government waste a lot of money we pay in taxes,
_____ waste some of it, or not very much? 1. not much 2. some 3. a lot 4. no opinion

23). How much time do you think you can trust the government in Washington to do
_____ what is right? 1. always 2. most of the time 3. some of the time 4. never

24). Would you say that the government is pretty much run by a few big interests
looking out for themselves or that it is run for the benefit of all the people?
_____ 1. for benefit of all 2. few big interests 3. no opinion

25). Do you think that quite a few of the people running the government are
_____ crooked, not very many, or hardly any? 1. hardly any 2. not many 3. quite a few

26). Do you belong to any other political groups or organizations (including any
_____ other pro-life organizations)? 1. yes 2. no

_____ 27). Do you consider yourself a: 1. liberal 2. conservative 3. moderate
4. other_____.

For each of the following items below, indicate your feelings, positive or negative, using the following scale: 1=very positive; 2=somewhat positive; 3=neutral;
4=somewhat negative; 5=very negative; 6=don't know or no opinion.

____Moral Majority   ____Ronald Reagan
____Mario Cuomo   ____Alphonse D'Amato
____Daniel P. Moynihan   ____Jerry Falwell
____Jimmy Carter   ____Edward Kennedy

_____Walter Mondale
_____James Watt
_____Thomas P. "Tip" O'Neill
_____Phyllis Schlafly
_____Henry Kissinger
_____having a death penalty in New
York

_____George Bush
_____George Wallace
_____National Rifle Association
_____Equal Rights Amendment
_____Supreme Court
_____Richard Nixon

Why did you decide to enroll in the Right to Life Party?_____

_____

_____

_____

How do you think the Right to Life Party can best promote the right to life

objective?_____

_____

_____ 28). What is your marital status? 1. single 2. married

_____ 29). How many grades of school did you finish (if you are still in school, put
down the last year you have finished, with an "X" before the number)? 1. grade
school only 2. some high school 3. high school graduate (or equivalent) 4. some
college 5. college graduate 5. graduate school

_____ 30). What is your age?

_____ 31). Do you have any children? 1. yes 2. no

_____ 32). If "yes," how many?

_____ 33). Sex: 1. male 2. female

_____ 34). What is your religious affiliation? 1. Catholic 2. Protestant 3. Jewish
4. Mormon 5. not religious 6. other

35). If Protestant, any particular denomination?_____.

_____ 36). How often would you say you go to church? 1. every week 2. almost every
week 3. once or twice a month 4. a few times a year 5. never

37). What is your occupation?_____.

_____ 38). Are you a member of a union? 1. yes 2. no

39). If "yes," what union?_____.

_____ 40). How many years have you lived in New York State?

_____ 41). What is your total family income? 1. under $5,000 2. $5,000-9,999 3. $10,000-
14,999 4. $15,000-19,999 5. $20,000-24,999 6. $25,000-29,999 7. $30,000+

THANK YOU!

Right to Life Party Enrollment, 1984*

County	Number of Enrolled RTLP Members	County	Number of Enrolled RTLP Members
Albany	212	Ontario	102
Allegany	72	Orange	282
Broome	142	Orleans	31
Cattaraugus	160	Oswego	131
Cayuga	84	Otsego	77
Chautauqua	231	Putnam	118
Chemung	95	Rensselaer	340
Chenango	80	Rockland	569
Clinton	55	St. Lawrence	75
Columbia	73	Saratoga	132
Cortland	56	Schenectady	200
Delaware	40	Schoharie	37
Dutchess	484	Schuyler	24
Erie	1,708	Seneca	47
Essex	30	Steuben	109
Franklin	33	Suffolk	1,923
Fulton	48	Sullivan	94
Genesee	65	Tioga	59
Greene	42	Tompkins	60
Hamilton	7	Ulster	243
Herkimer	44	Warren	35
Jefferson	67	Washington	32
Lewis	23	Wayne	86
Livingston	66	Westchester	1,242
Madison	66	Wyoming	45
Monroe	960	Yates	16
Montgomery	58	Bronx	723
Nassau	1,837	Kings	1,764
Niagara	331	New York	513
Oneida	315	Queens	1,361
Onondaga	595	Richmond	384
		Total	18,933

*Other statewide party enrollment totals: Democrat - 3,548,858; Republican - 2.470,836; Conservative - 107,995; Liberal - 65,031; blank, void, missing - 1,302,419.

BIBLIOGRAPHY

The Alan Guttmacher Institute. *Safe and Legal: 10 Years' Experience with Legal Abortion in New York State.* New York: The Alan Guttmacher Institute, 1980.

The American Assembly, Columbia University. "The Future of American Political Parties." Sixty-Second American Assembly, April 15–18, 1982, Arden House, Harriman, NY.

Barnartt, Sharon N., and Richard J. Harris. "Recent Changes in Predictors of Abortion Attitudes." *Sociology and Social Research* 66 (1982), 320–34.

"The Battle over Abortion." *Time,* April 6, 1981, pp. 20–28.

Beatty, Kathleen M., and Oliver Walter. "Religious Preference and Practice: Reevaluating Their Impact on Political Tolerance." *Public Opinion Quarterly* 48 (Spring, 1984), 318–29.

Behn, Dick. "Liberals and Conservatives: The Importance of New York's Two 'Third' Parties." *Empire State Report* (April, 1977), 164–69.

Blackman, Paul H. *Third Party President?* Washington, DC: Heritage Foundation, 1976.

Blake, Judith. "Abortion and Public Opinion: The 1960–1970 Decade." *Science* 71 (February, 1971), 540–49.

Blake, Judith, and Jorge H. Del Pinal. "Predicting Polar Attitudes Toward Abortion in the United States." *Abortion Parley.* Edited by James T. Burtchaell. Kansas City, KA: Andrews and McMeel, Inc., 1980.

―――. "Negativism, Equivocation, and Wobbly Assent." *Demography* 18, 3 (1981), 309–20.

Blocker, Jack S., Jr. *Retreat from Reform: The Prohibition Movement in the United States, 1880–1913.* Westport, CT: Greenwood Press, 1976.

Blue, Frederick. *The Free Soilers*. Urbana, IL: University of Illinois Press, 1973.

Brady, David W., and Kent L. Tedin. "Ladies in Pink: Religion and Political Ideology in the Anti-ERA Movement." *Social Science Quarterly* (March, 1976), 564–75.

Brams, Steven J., and Peter Fishburn. *Approval Voting*. Boston: Birkhauser, 1983.

Broder, David. *The Party's Over*. New York: Harper and Row, 1971.

Buck, Solon J. *The Agrarian Crusade*. New Haven, CT: Yale University Press, 1921.

Burnham, Walter Dean. *Critical Elections*. New York: W. W. Norton, 1970.

Califano, Joseph A. *Governing America*. New York: Simon and Schuster, 1981.

Callahan, Daniel. *Abortion: Law, Choice and Morality*. New York: Macmillan, 1970.

Carmines, Edward G., and James A. Stimson. "The Two Faces of Issue Voting." *American Political Science Review* 74, 1 (March, 1980), 78–91.

Chambers, William N., and Walter Dean Burnham. *The American Party System*. New York: Oxford University Press, 1975.

Clark, Norman. *Deliver Us from Evil: An Interpretation of American Prohibition*. New York: W. W. Norton, 1976.

Colvin, David L. *Prohibition in the United States: A History of the Prohibition Party, and of the Prohibition Movement*. New York: Doran, 1926.

The Committee on Responsible Parties, American Political Science Association. *Toward a More Responsible Two-Party System*. New York: Rinehart and Co., 1950.

Conover, Pamela Johnston. "The Mobilization of the New Right: A Test of Various Explanations." *Western Political Quarterly* (December, 1983), 632–49.

Conover, Pamela Johnston, and Stanley Feldman. "The Origins and Meaning of Liberal/Conservative Self-Identifications." *American Journal of Political Science* 25, 4 (November, 1981), 617–45.

Conover, Pamela Johnston, and Virginia Gray. *Feminism and the New Right: Conflict over the American Family*. New York: Praeger, 1983.

Conover, Pamela Johnston, Steve Coombs, and Virginia Gray. "The Attitudinal Roots of Single-Issue Politics: The Case of 'Women's Issues.' " A paper presented at the 1980 Annual Meeting of the American Political Science Association, the Washington Hilton Hotel, Washington, DC, August 28–31.

"The Constitutionality of Anti-Fusion and Party-Raiding Statutes." *Columbia Law Review* 47 (1947).

Converse, Philip. "The Nature of Belief Systems in Mass Publics." *Ideology and Discontent*. Edited by David Apter. New York: Free Press, 1964.

———. "Change in the American Electorate." *The Human Meaning of Social Change*. Edited by Angus Campbell and Philip Converse. New York: Russell Sage Foundation, 1972.

Crotty, William. *American Parties in Decline*. Boston: Little, Brown, 1984.

Dillon, Merton L. *The Abolitionists*. DeKalb, IL: Northern Illinois University Press, 1974.

Dodd, Lawrence C. *Coalitions in Parliamentary Governments*. Princeton, NJ: Princeton University Press, 1976.

Duverger, Maurice.*Political Parties*. New York: Wiley, 1954.

Ellwood, John W. "A Model of the Life-Cycle of American Minor Parties." A paper presented at the 1977 Annual Meeting of the Southern Political Science Association, New Orleans, LA, November 5.

Ellwood, John W., and Robert J. Spitzer. "The Democratic National Telethons." *Journal of Politics* 41, 3 (August, 1979), 828–64.

Elms, Alan C. "Psychological Factors in Right-Wing Extremism." *The American Right Wing*. Edited by Robert A. Schoenberger. New York: Holt, Rinehart and Winston, 1969.

Epstein, Leon D. "The Scholarly Commitment to Parties." *Political Science: The State of the Discipline*. Edited by Ada W. Finifter. Washington, DC: American Political Science Association, 1983.

Falik, Marilyn. *Ideology and Abortion Policy Politics*. New York: Praeger, 1983.

Feigert, Frank B. "Conservatism, Populism, and Social Change." *American Behavioral Scientist* 17, 2 (November/December, 1973), 272–78.

———. "Environmental Dynamics and Aggregate Voting Studies: Conservative Voting in New York." A paper presented at the Annual Meeting of the Southern Political Science Association, Atlanta, GA, November 2–4, 1972.

Fine, Nathan. *Labor and Farmer Parties in the United States: 1828–1928*. New York: Rand School of Social Science, 1928.

Fishel, Jeff, ed. *Parties and Elections in an Anti-Party Age*. Bloomington, IN: Indiana University Press, 1978.

Fleishman, Joel L., ed. *The Future of American Political Parties*. Englewood Cliffs, NJ: Prentice-Hall, 1982.

Francke, Linda Bird. *The Ambivalence of Abortion*. New York: Random House, 1978.

Frohock, Fred M. *Abortion: A Case Study in Law and Morals*. Westport, CT: Greenwood Press, 1983.

Gallup Report. "Attitudes Toward Abortion Have Changed Little Since Mid–70s." *Gallup Report* (June, 1980), 6–7.

Gelb, Joyce, and Marian L. Palley. "Women and Interest Group Politics: A Comparative Analysis of Federal Decision-Making." *Journal of Politics* 41, 2 (May, 1979), 262–92.

———. *Women and Public Policies*. Princteon, NJ: Princeton University Press, 1982.

Gibson, James L., et al. "Assessing Party Organizational Strength." *American Journal of Political Science* 27, 2 (May, 1983), 193–222.

Ginsberg, Benjamin. *The Consequences of Consent*. Reading, MA: Addison-Wesley, 1982.

———. "Elections and Public Policy." *American Political Science Review* (March, 1976), 41–49.

Gitelson, Alan, M. Margaret Conway, and Frank B. Feigert. *American Political Parties: Stability and Change*. Boston: Houghton Mifflin, 1984.

Granberg, Donald. "The Abortion Activists." *Family Planning Perspectives* 13, 4 (July/August, 1981), 157–63.

———. "Pro-Life or Reflections of Conservative Ideology? An Analysis of Opposition to Legalized Abortion." *Sociology and Social Research* 62, 3 (Winter, 1977/1978), 414–29.

Gray, Virginia, Herbert Jacob, and Kenneth N. Vines, eds. *Politics in the American States*. 4th Ed. Boston: Little, Brown, 1983.

Gusfield, Joseph R. *Symbolic Crusade*. Urbana, IL: University of Illinois Press, 1963.

Haynes, Fred E. *Third Party Movements Since the Civil War with Special Reference to Iowa*. Iowa City, IA: State Historical Society, 1916.

Hesseltine, William B. *The Rise and Fall of Third Parties*. Washington, DC: Public Affairs Press, 1948.

———. *Third Party Movements in the United States*. New York: Van Nostrand, 1962.

Hofstedter, Richard. *The Idea of a Party System*. Berkeley, CA: University of California Press, 1955.

Jaffe, Frederick S., Barbara L. Lindheim, and Philip R. Lee. *Abortion Politics: Private Morality and Public Policy*. New York: McGraw-Hill, 1981.

Jain, Sagar C. and Laurel F. Gooch. *Georgia Abortion Act 1968*. Chapel Hill, NC: University of North Carolina, School of Public Health, 1972.

Jain, Sagar C., and Steven Hughes. *California Abortion Act 1967*. Chapel Hill, NC: University of North Carolina, Carolina Population Center, 1969.

Jain, Sagar C., and Steven W. Sinding. *North Carolina Abortion Law 1967*. Chapel Hill, NC: University of North Carolina Press, 1968.

Johnston, Michael. "The 'New Christian Right' in American Politics." *The Political Quarterly* 53, 2 (April-June, 1982), 181–99.

Karen, Robert. "The Politics of Pressure." *The Nation*, September 20, 1975, pp,. 235–40.

Kayden, Xandra, and Eddie Mahe, Jr. *The Party Goes On.* New York: Basic Books, 1985.

Key, V. O. "Secular Realignment and the Party System." *Journal of Politics* 21 (May, 1959), 198–210.

Kirkpatrick, Jeane J. *Dismantling the Parties.* Washington, DC: American Enterprise Institute, 1978.

Kleppner, Paul, et al. *The Evolution of American Electoral Systems.* Westport, CT: Greenwood Press, 1981.

Ladd, Everett C. *Where Have All the Voters Gone?* New York: W. W. Norton, 1982.

Liebman, Robert C., and Robert Wuthnow, eds. *The New Christian Right.* Hawthorne, New York: Aldine Publishing, 1983.

Lienesch, Michael. "Right-Wing Religion: Christian Conservatism as a Political Movement." *Political Science Quarterly* 97, 3 (Fall, 1982), 403–25.

Lowi, Theodore J. "Toward a More Responsible Three-Party System." *PS* 16, 4 (Fall, 1983), 699–706.

Lubell, Samuel. *The Future of American Politics.* New York: Doubleday, 1956.

Luker, Kristin. *Abortion and the Politics of Motherhood.* Berkeley, CA: University of California Press, 1984.

Luttbeg, Norman. "The Structure of Beliefs Among Leaders and the Public." *Public Opinion Quarterly* 32 (Fall, 1968), 398–409.

Margolis, Michael, and Kevin Neary. "Pressure Politics Revisited: The Anti-Abortion Campaign." *Policy Studies Journal* 8 (Spring, 1980), 698–717.

Mazmanian, Daniel A. *Third Parties in Presidential Elections.* Washington, DC: Brookings Institution, 1974.

McCormick, E. Patricia. *Attitudes Toward Abortion.* Lexington, MA: Lexington Books, 1975.

Merton, Andrew H. *Enemies of Choice.* Boston: Beacon Press, 1981.

Milbrath, Lester. *Political Participation.* Chicago: Rand McNally, 1965.

Miller, Arthur H., and Martin P. Wattenberg. "Politics from the Pulpit: Religiosity and the 1980 Elections." *Public Opinion Quarterly* 48 (Spring, 1984), 301–17.

Miller, Tim. "Two Competing 'Pro-Life' Measures Split the Anti-Abortion Lobby." *National Journal*, March 20, 1982, pp. 511–13.

Mohr, James C. *Abortion in America.* New York: Oxford University Press, 1978.

Moscow, Warren. *Politics in the Empire State.* New York: Knopf, 1948.

Mueller, Carol. "In Search of a Constituency for the 'New Religious Right.' " *Public Opinion Quarterly* 47 (Summer, 1983), 213–29.

Nash, Howard P. *Third Parties in American Politics.* Washington, DC: Public Affairs Press, 1959.

Nelson, Michael, ed. *The Elections of 1984.* Washington, DC: Congressional Quarterly Press, 1985.

Nie, Norman H., Sidney Verba, and John R. Petrocik. *The Changing American Voter.* Cambridge: Harvard University Press, 1976.

Noonan, John. *A Private Choice: Abortion in America in the Seventies.* New York: Free Press, 1979.

Paige, Connie. *The Right to Lifers.* New York: Summit Books, 1983.

Patterson, Samuel C., and Gregory A. Caldeira. "The Etiology of Partisan Competition." *American Political Science Reveiw* 78, 3 (September, 1984), 691–707.

Penniman, Howard R. "Presidential Third Parties and the Modern American Two-Party System." *The Party Symbol.* Edited by William Crotty. San Francisco: W. W. Freeman, 1980.

Peterson, Larry R., and Armand L. Mauss. "Religion and the 'Right to Life'—Correlates of Opposition to Abortion." *Sociological Analysis* 37 (1976), 243–54.

Polsby, Nelson. *Consequences of Party Reform.* New York: Oxford University Press, 1983.

Pomper, Gerald. *Elections in America.* New York: Dodd, Mead, 1968.

Pomper, Gerald, ed. *Party Renewal in America.* New York: Praeger, 1980.

Powell, G. Bingham. "Party Systems and Political System Performance." *American Political Science Review* 75, 4 (December, 1981), 861–79.

President's Commission for a National Agenda for the Eighties. *The Electoral and Democratic Process in the Eighties.* Paul G. Rogers, Chairperson. Englewood Cliffs, NJ: Prentice-Hall, 1981.

Price, David E. *Bringing Back the Parties.* Washington, DC: Congressional Quarterly Press, 1984.

Ranney, Austin. *Curing the Mischiefs of Faction.* Berkeley, CA: University of California Press, 1975.

———. *The Doctrine of Responsible Party Government.* Urbana, IL: University of Illinois Press, 1954.

Ranney, Austin, and Willmoore Kendall. *Democracy and the American Party System.* New York: Harcourt, Brace, 1956.

———. "Parties in State Politics," *Politics in the American States.* Edited by Herbert Jacob and Kenneth Vines, 2nd edition. Boston: Little, Brown, 1971.

Rayback, Joseph G. *Free Soil: The Election of 1848.* Lexington, KY: University of Kentucky Press, 1970.

Reagan, Ronald. *Abortion and the Conscience of a Nation*. Nashville: Thomas Nelson Publishers, 1984.

Rockwood, D. Stephen, et al. *American Third Parties Since the Civil War*. New York: Garland Publishing, 1985.

Rosenstone, Steven J., Roy Behr, and Edward Lazarus. *Third Parties in America*. Princeton, NJ: Princeton University Press, 1984.

Rossiter, Clinton. *Parties and Politics in America*. Ithaca, NY: Cornell University Press, 1960.

Rubin, Eva R. *Abortion, Politics, and the Courts*. Westport, CT: Greenwood Press, 1982.

Saltman, Jules, and Stanley Zimmering. *Abortion Today*. Springfield, IL: Thomas, 1973.

Sartori, Giovanni. *Parties and Party Systems*. New York: Cambridge University Press, 1976.

Scarrow, Howard A. *Parties, Elections, and Representation in the State of New York*. New York: New York University Press, 1983.

————. "The Strength of New York's Political Parties." A paper presented at the Annual Meeting of the New York State Political Science Association, Albany, NY, April 6–7, 1984.

Schattschneider, E. E. *Party Government*. New York: Holt, Rinehart and Winston, 1942.

Schlesinger, Joseph A. "The New American Political Party." A paper presented at the 1984 Annual Meeting of the American Political Science Association, the Washington Hilton, Washington, DC, August 30–September 2.

Schneider, Carl E., and Maris A. Vinovskis, eds. *The Law and Politics of Abortion*. Lexington, MA: Lexington Books, 1980.

Schoenberger, Robert A. "Conservatism, Personality and Political Extremism." *American Political Science Review* 62, 3 (September, 1968), 868–77.

Scott, Ruth K., and Ronald J. Hrebenar. *Parties in Crisis*. New York: Wiley, 1984.

Sewell, Richard H. *Ballots for Freedom*. New York: Oxford University Press, 1976.

Singh, B. Krishna, and Peter J. Leghy. "Contextual and Ideological Dimensions of Attitudes Toward Discretionary Abortion." *Demography* 15, 3 (1978), 381–88.

"Single Issue Politics." *Newsweek*, November 8, 1978, pp. 48–60.

Skerry, Peter. "The Class Conflict Over Abortion." *The Public Interest* 52 (Summer, 1978), 69–84.

Smallwood, Frank. *The Other Candidates*. Hanover, NH: University Press of New England, 1983.

Smelser, Neil J. *Theory of Collective Behavior*. New York: Free Press, 1963.

"Special Report." *Newsweek*, October 8, 1979, pp. 46–48.

Spitzer, Robert J. "A Political Party Is Born: Single-Issue Advocacy and the Election Law in New York State." *National Civic Review* (July/August, 1984), 321–28.

———. "The Tail Wagging the Dog: Multi-Party Politics." *New York State Today*. Edited by Peter W. Colby. Albany, NY: SUNY Press, 1985.

Stedman, Murray S., and Susan Stedman. *Discontent at the Polls*. New York: Russell and Russell, 1967.

Steiner, Gilbert Y., ed. *The Abortion Dispute and the American System*. Washington, DC: Brookings Institution, 1983.

Steinhoff, Patricia, and Milton Diamond. *Abortion Politics: The Hawaii Experience*. Honolulu: University Press of Hawaii, 1977.

Storms, Roger C. *Partisan Prophets: A History of the Prohibition Party, 1854–1972*. Denver: National Prohibition Foundation, 1972.

Sundquist, James L. *Dynamics of the Party System*. Washington, DC: Brookings Institution, 1983.

———. "Whither the American Party System?—Revisited." *Political Science Quarterly* (Winter, 1983–84), 573–93.

Tatalovich, Raymond, and Byron W. Daynes. "Moral Controversies and the Policymaking Process." *Policy Studies Review* (February, 1984), 203–19.

———. *The Politics of Abortion*. New York: Praeger, 1981.

Tedrow, Lucky M., and E. R. Mahoney. "Trends in Attitudes Toward Abortion." *Public Opinion Quarterly* 43 (Summer, 1979), 181–89.

Tesh, Sylvia. "In Support of 'Single-Issue' Politics." *Political Science Quarterly* 99, 2 (Spring, 1984), 27–44.

Timberlake, James H. *Prohibition and the Progressive Movement*. Cambridge: Harvard University Press, 1963.

Unger, Irwin. *The Greenback Era: A Social and Political History of American Finance, 1865–1879*. Princeton, NJ: Princeton University Press, 1964.

Useem, Michael. *Protest Movements in America*. Indianapolis: Bobbs-Merrill, 1975.

Verba, Sidney, and Norman Nie. *Participation in America*. New York: Harper and Row, 1972.

Wattenberg, Martin P. *The Decline of American Political Parties, 1952–1980*. Cambridge: Harvard University Press, 1984.

Williams, Roger N. "The Power of Fetal Politics." *Saturday Review*, June 9, 1979, pp. 12–15.

Zald, Mayer N., and John D. McCarthy, eds. *The Dynamics of Social Movements*. Cambridge: Winthrop, 1979.

Zimmerman, Joseph F. *The Government and Politics of New York State*. New York: New York University Press, 1981.

INDEX

Abolition of alcohol. *See*
  Prohibition
Abolition of slavery, 6, 8, 10, 13,
  17, 22, 29
Abortion: attitudes, determinants
  of, 54–55; and constitutional
  convention, 70; educational
  efforts, 56; grassroots
  beginnings, 58; hard vs. soft
  conditions for allowing, 54;
  issue intensity, 56; liberalized
  practices, 40, 58, 67; political
  action committees, 56, 70, 79
  n.57, 80 n.61; practices in New
  York, 39–40; public opinion,
  39–41, 54, 74 n.9, 76 n.30, 77
  n.31, 78 n.47, 81; religion, 82–
  83, 104 n.17; single-issue, 1, 2,
  39, 79 n.55, 100, 101; social
  issue, 39; social unrest, 57;
  state controversy, 40; Supreme
  Court decisions, 76 n.28;
  violence, 2, 57
Adams, Charles Francis, 15
American Antislavery Society, 6,
  7
American Assembly, 116
American Labor Party (ALP), 45,
  48

American Political Science
  Association Committee on
  Political Parties, 114
Anderson, Don Benny, 1
Anderson, John, 86, 117
Anti-Monopoly Party, 21
Anti-party sentiment, 9
Anti-Saloon League (ASL), 25,
  26, 28, 36 n.125
Antislavery movement: internal
  conflicts, 10; parties, 6;
  societies, 6
Approval voting, 124
Army of God, 1, 57

Ballot access, New York, 41
Ballot position, New York, 74
  n.10
Barnburners, 12, 13, 15
Behr, Roy, 50
Birney, James G., 7, 8, 9, 10, 11,
  14
Blackmail, electoral, 60
Bohner, Robert, 62, 88
Brady, David W., 96
Brown, Paul, 53
Buckley, James, 43
Bush, George, 61
Butler, Benjamin F., 21

ABOUT THE AUTHOR

ROBERT J. SPITZER is an Associate Professor and Department Chair of the Political Science Department at the State University of New York College at Cortland. His interests include political parties and elections, the American presidency, state government and politics, the legislative process, policymaking and mass media. He is also the author of *The Presidency and Public Policy: The Four Arenas of Presidential Power* (1983). His articles have appeared in various volumes of edited readings, and also in the *Journal of Politics, Presidential Studies Quarterly,* the *National Civic Review, America* and several newspapers.